W9-AAY-843

People socializing and dating on the Internet often have different reasons for wanting to meet others. Here are the five most common types of people, based on their social objectives.

The Dabbler has gone online to "see what this Internet dating thing is all about," but doesn't usually have any plan other than "to have fun." As you begin your journey socializing with others over the Net, you might find yourself in the middle of an email or chat room conversation that you thought was going really well, when the other party goes AWOL. That's the dabbler either getting bored or realizing that connection with another individual is not really what he or she is after.

The Nester wants to find a committed relationship and is looking to the Internet as one of many ways to find one. He or she is usually very goal-oriented in that the purpose of socializing online is not about the process of forging friendships, but is about finding THE ONE PERSON that will be his or her lifetime mate.

The Hormone wants sex. Usually he or she will make this very clear early on. Hormones vary in that some just want virtual sex (that is, simulating sex via a private chat room discussion or email), some want to meet you in the physical world, and some want it in all manner, shape, and form.

The Butterfly goes from chat room to chat room, person to person, having conversations with a multitude of different people. He or she is looking to make one or more friends and usually keeps the relationship platonic. In a simpler time, this person went by the name pen pal.

The Seeker doesn't know what he or she is looking for, but unlike the Dabbler, is seeking to make some sort of connection with another person. He or she might claim to be looking for a partner or just looking for sex, but the actual agenda is usually unknown to the Seeker.

Emoticons

Emoticon	Description
:) or :-)	The original smiley that means "I'm happy." Can also mean "I'm joking."
:(or :-(	"I'm sad." Indicates to the reader that the current writer is sad at what he or she has just heard.
;-)	A wink. Usually used for a flirtatious or sarcastic remark.
{hug} or [hug]	A hug.
{{{***}}}	Hugs and kisses.

If you'd like to explore the hundreds (if not thousands) of emoticons currently being used (or if you need to find the meaning of one), you can check out the following resources:

Online Lingo   `http://www.thirdage.com/features/tech/netglos/index.html`
Internet Smileys.... ^_^   `http://members.aol.com/bearpage/smileys.htm`
Smilies Unlimited   `http://www.czweb.com/smilies.htm`

cut here

Acronyms that are common to the Internet have made their way into the messages people use to socialize online. Some of the more widely used ones are:

Acronym	Meaning
AFAIK	As far as I know
A/S/L	Age/Sex/Location
BBL	Be back later
BTW	By the way
DIKY	Do I know you?
GAL	Get a life
ILY	I love you
F2F	Face to face
IRL	In real life
LOL	Laugh out loud

If you want to learn and decipher the hundreds of additional acronyms found online, check out the following resources:

Alphabet Soup Explained `http://members.aol.com/nigthomas/alphabet.html`
Usenet Acronyms Dictionary `http://homepages.ihug.co.nz/~tajwileb/`
`dictionary.html`
V.E.R.A. (Virtual Entity of Relevant Acronyms) `http://userpage.`
`fu-berlin.de/~oheiabbd/vera-e.html` (This is a search engine for acronyms.)

Do You Hate to Type?

Would you rather just click a link to visit the Web sites in this book? Just point your browser to

`http://www.size-eight.com/book`

This site provides links to every Web page discussed in *The Complete Idiot's Guide to Online Dating and Relating* as well as new socializing Web sites that were created after this book went to press.

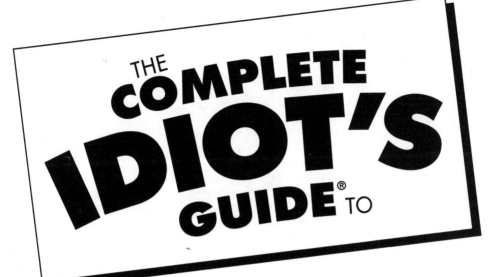

THE **COMPLETE IDIOT'S GUIDE**® TO

Online Dating and Relating

Joe Schwartz

A Division of Macmillan USA
201 West 103rd Street, Indianapolis, Indiana 46290

The Complete Idiot's Guide to Online Dating and Relating

International Standard Book Number: 0-7897-2169-4

Library of Congress Catalog Card Number: 99-63407

Printed in the United States of America

First Printing: November 1999

01   00   99   4   3   2   1

Trademarks

Warning and Disclaimer

Associate Publisher
Greg Wiegand

Acquisitions Editor
Angelina Ward

Development Editor
Sarah Robbins

Managing Editor
Thomas F. Hayes

Technical Editor
Robert E. Patrick

Illustrator
Judd Winick

Project Editor
Lori A. Lyons

Copy Editor
Sossity Smith

Indexer
Kevin Broccoli

Proofreader
Tricia Sterling

Team Coordinator
Sharry Gregory

Interior Designer
Nathan Clement

Cover Designer
Michael Freeland

Copy Writer
Eric Borgert

Production
Dan Harris
Cyndi Davis-Hubler

Contents at a Glance

Contents

Part 4: I've Had a Hard Day — 195

15 When a Door Closes, It Gets Dark — 197

16 There's More to Venting Than Duct Tape — 207

17 Me, Myself, and I — 217

Dedication

For my mother, without whose dating and relating skills I would not exist.

Acknowledgments

First and foremost, I'd like to thank the makers of the Quasar Cool Look air conditioner. Mostly written during one of the hottest summers in New York City history, this book would not have been possible without the Cool Look's dulcet sputtering. Even as I write this, my ever-trusty frigid friend is maintaining a relatively balmy 80 degrees inside my small apartment as urbanites scurry to take shelter from the 104-degree swelter outside my window. I know, you're thinking an air conditioner should probably do a slightly better job. But the Cool Look and I have a long and storied history of surviving the indignities of these past seven New York summers. I fear this shall be our last campaign together, the clanking of its fan a little too loud, the exhalation of its breath a bit too shallow. Were it not for the existence of my mother, I would have dedicated this book to the Cool Look.

I would also like to thank Cynthia Marsh for bringing me to the attention of Macmillan USA; Angelina Ward, Sarah Robbins, Sharry Gregory, and the other hard-working employees of Macmillan for laboring to bring this book to press; Judd Winick for his input and for creating this text's illustrations; Dennis Barsky, Drake Colley, Sheri Rosenberg, Byron Ricks, and Sandy Miller for freely offering me their wisdom and counsel; all of my anonymous "From the Frontlines" contributors for submitting their touching, funny, and painful online dating anecdotes; Joe Simko for sharing his immense talents with Size Eight; Gary Barsky, Dave Brown, Andy Erdman, Rob Handelman, David Leonard (who still can't smell the Internet), Karen Miller, and Stacy and Todd Powell for their love, friendship, and unwavering support; Jim Spero and Osei Ofosu-Benefo for the good vibe; and Fern, Myron, Spencer, Jordan, and Heather for being there for me. Lastly, I'd like to thank a group of people who, for the most part, I rarely see or are no longer in contact with, but whose impact on my life has been, and always will be, immeasurable. They are Bob Kent, Russ Ratsch, Morton Kaplan, Glen Eichenblatt, Bob Sturmer, Gil Valdes, Vicki Hart, and Al Sharf.

Tell Us What You Think!

As the reader of this book, *you* are our most important critic and commentator. We value your opinion and want to know what we're doing right, what we could do better, what areas you'd like to see us publish in, and any other words of wisdom you're willing to pass our way.

As an Associate Publisher for Que, I welcome your comments. You can fax, email, or write me directly to let me know what you did or didn't like about this book—as well as what we can do to make our books stronger.

Please note that I cannot help you with technical problems related to the topic of this book, and that due to the high volume of mail I receive, I might not be able to reply to every message.

When you write, please be sure to include this book's title and author as well as your name and phone or fax number. I will carefully review your comments and share them with the author and editors who worked on the book.

Fax: 317.581.4666

Email: office_que@mcp.com

Mail: Greg Wiegand
         Que
         201 West 103rd Street
         Indianapolis, IN 46290 USA

Introduction

"You can't smell the Internet." Or so says my friend Dave as he canoodles on his living room couch with his steady. Yet, what he and many other members of happy couples don't see is how hard it is to meet someone in the non-cyber world. With every person having a unique set of needs and desires, it's no wonder that some of the great thinkers of all time have labeled the act of connecting with another individual as one of the hardest things to accomplish in life. Yet, the Internet can help you meet whatever interpersonal goals you might have: friendship or companionship, activity partnering or casual dating, marriage or life commitment. All these possibilities and more exist. And yes, if you're looking for sex, that, too, is ever-present in an amazing range of proclivities.

What makes the online world so ideal for matters of the heart is that it puts you in control of some of the most basic elements of human interaction:

- You can remain anonymous for as long as you deem necessary, allowing you to explore relationships freely and in safety.
- You can be as specific or nonspecific as you like in your criteria for a partner vis-à-vis religion, geography, sexual preference, race, personal values, and other issues.
- You can do it all from the comfort of your home, making even a bad hair day a productive interpersonal experience.
- You can save time by avoiding face-to-face liaisons with people who are clearly not going to be compatible with you.

As I write this, we probably have a few things in common: We're both looking to meet someone, we don't look like models or advertisements for "The Night of the Living Dead," and despite the onslaught of blame we received in childhood, neither of us has cooties. So, I suggest that we explore the online world of interpersonal interaction together. Who knows, perhaps that smell of cologne or perfume wafting from your couch several weeks from now will be the smell of the Internet.

How to Use This Book

This book has been divided into five parts so that you can find the information you need regardless of whether you are looking to date, get married, make online friends, or fulfill any of the uncountable interpersonal goals that people pursue.

Part 1, "All Alone with a Warm Box," prepares you for online socializing by exploring these topics: the types of people already reaching out to others on the Internet; the hardware and software you'll need to communicate with them; and the steps you should take to keep yourself safe while exploring those relationships.

Part 2, "Dating Bytes," is geared towards helping you meet others online with the goal of moving those relationships into the offline world. It begins with suggestions on how to prepare a personal ad for posting online; an introduction to cyber-flirting using Internet abbreviations and other methods; and a tour of dozens of personal ad Web sites. It ends with a chapter devoted to sites designed to help you woo someone online and another featuring sites with humorous, as well as serious, relationship advice.

Part 3, "I Just Want Someone I Can Talk To," explores the various venues for finding and maintaining online friendships. Two chapters are devoted to online chat with instant messaging, message boards and newsgroups, and unusual sites and technologies for conversing with people each getting an additional chapter. Should any of these friendships turn into a lifelong commitment, a chapter on Web sites that help you plan your wedding online is also included.

Part 4, "I've Had a Hard Day," will help you cope with the end of an online or offline relationship, should this happen. Web sites that deal with breaking up, divorce, and just venting about one gender or another are all featured. This part of the book concludes with a chapter featuring sites that assist you in the most important relationship you will ever have: the one with yourself.

Part 5, "Has Anyone Seen My Magic Eight Ball?," takes a look at Web sites that try to predict your future, romantic and otherwise. It ends with the author's own predictions for the future of online dating and relating.

How Do You Use This Book?

To help make the world of Internet socializing easier, this book features anecdotes from people who have already tested the online dating waters, as well as warnings and informational tips to assist you while meeting people online. These illustrated extras appear in these boxes:

From the Frontlines

These great asides are anecdotes from those who have already dated people they met online.

Tips

Tips provide extra bits of information concerning the personal or technical aspects of dating and relating online.

Warnings

Cautionary information helps you steer clear of embarrassing or dangerous online situations.

Part 1

All Alone with a Warm Box

You and your computer. Although the two of you probably make a nice-looking couple, this first part of The Complete Idiot's Guide to Online Dating and Relating *is designed to expand that relationship by preparing you to include into it others who you meet on the Internet. First, we'll explore the types of people you might meet and what their agendas might be. Next, we'll quickly discuss the computer hardware and software you'll need for online socializing. Finally, we'll explore methods for keeping yourself safe and anonymous while interacting with new people online, as well as precautions to take when meeting someone offline for the first time.*

Chapter 1

Hey, Nice Keyboard!

In This Chapter

➤ Explore the fear of online socializing

➤ Learn how long online socializing has been going on

➤ Learn who is looking to meet you online

➤ Learn about people's agendas online

These Boots Were Made for Quaking

When I first started thinking about meeting people online I was the proverbial white knuckle. Wasn't it well known that all those Internet nerds are just Unibombers waiting to explode? Or ruthless lotharios looking to prey on the innocent? What about all the pornographers and sexual predators? Even worse, what would happen if the people I actually know find out!?! Would they label me as (please, please anything but this!) desperate? There was little I could do to keep the mouse from shaking out of my hand. But as I started to look at people's personal ads, listen to their thoughts via chat rooms, and encounter them in the real world after online interchanges, I discovered the only real truism of online dating and relating: everybody's scared. Here are a few samples from recent personal ads:

> *"I can't believe I'm doing this…"*
>
> *"I'm not the kind of guy who needs to go on the internet to find a date, as I am very attractive and there are always women who want to go out with me. However…"*
>
> *"My mother suggested I place this ad online…"*
>
> *"If you're a loser, nutjob, creep or even a bigger loser, DO NOT read on!"*

All these quotes reflect the fact that everyone is afraid of getting hurt. No one likes to feel rejection or embarrassment on one end of the spectrum or pain, either emotionally or physically, on the other. And that is exactly the reason why the Internet is the perfect means for meeting someone: It leaves you in control of the amount of risk you want to take. As a relationship develops online, you can choose what information to divulge and when to do so. And, with the proper precautions, it can actually become a safer environment for dating than the random chance meetings, social functions, and setups from friends and relatives that are the staples of meeting someone in the real world.

But Who Is Really Out There?

Many of us have heard the statistics (more than 83 million U.S. citizens are on the Internet as of this writing, according to MediaMark Research), but how many people are using the Internet as a social medium? Some informal research shows that it's widespread. A few minutes ago I did an online search for the word "dating" on HotBot, an Internet search engine, that yielded 352,960 matching Web sites on that topic. Match.com, one of the most successful and popular online dating sites, claims that (as of this writing) more than 1.8 million people have used their service worldwide. Add to this the fact that almost every major Web-based community has one or more online areas devoted to helping people meet others, tells you that millions are using the Internet to socialize. In fact online socializing has been going on far longer and with much more widespread popularity than online commerce and investing.

Sheer Numbers

According to Nielsen Media Research, 760 American households join the Internet every hour. Although it is unknown how many of those households consist of or contain those looking to meet others, the sheer volume of people going online each day speaks well for the future of Internet socializing. (This fact, as well as others, can be found at Win Treese's Internet Index at `http://www.openmarket.com/intindex/index.cfm`.)

Just How Long Has Online Socializing Been Going On?

The beginnings of the Internet as we know it today started in 1969 when four major computers at different universities were connected by the Department of Defense's Advanced Research Projects Agency. And although in its infancy it was designed for computer experts, scientists, and researchers, it's not hard to imagine that it was also used for emails like the following:

> *Dear Martha:*
>
> *Just wanted to say how nice it was to see you again at the laser chromatography conference. Your new glasses make you look extremely attractive. (I can't believe two centimeters of thickness makes such a difference!) Perhaps when you're in town next I can show you my slide rule collection.*
>
> *Sincerely,*
>
> *Myron*

Of course, back then, the Internet was limited to mostly email and a few arcane technologies. It wasn't until 1979 when Tom Truscott and Jim Ellis, two graduate students at Duke University, and Steve Bellovin at the University of North Carolina, established the first Usenet newsgroups. These allowed people from all over the world to share ideas on literally thousands of topics. Unfortunately, this was great if you were a college student, but bad if you were a noncollegiate, because the Internet was still mostly accessed via universities. (Today these newsgroups are available to everyone; we'll learn about them in Chapter 12, "All the News That's Fit to Post.")

Since the advent of newsgroups, there has been no stopping people reaching out to others on the Internet. Most recently, the 1990s have brought about the advent of online commerce, graphical World Wide Web browsers, and major online services like America Online, all of which have led to more online socializing.

What Are People Looking For?

One of the most wonderful aspects of the Internet is that it allows people to be very specific about their likes and dislikes regarding who they want to come into contact with. Many people with very specific special-interests can often find others who share their passions. For example there's VeggieDate.com at `http://www.veggiedate.org`, which pairs up eligible vegetarians (see Figure 1.1). But for those who need their match to be vegetarian and Jewish there's Jewish Vegan/Vegetarian Singles at `http://www.jewishvegan.com/singlejvveg.html` (see Figure 1.2).

Figure 1.1

Vegetarians are just one of the many special interest groups that have their own dating site.

Figure 1.2

Even vegetarians can be broken up into smaller special interest groups as this site for Jewish vegetarian singles shows.

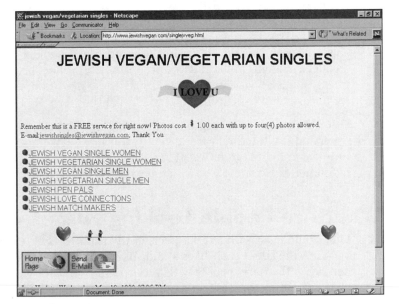

What Are They Really Looking For?

Putting aside matters of food choice, lifestyle, race, religion, sexual preference, and shared activities, people socializing and dating on the Internet have different agendas. I've divided the populace into five general categories.

The Dabbler

The Dabbler has gone online to "see what this Internet dating thing is all about," but doesn't usually have any plan other than "to have fun." As you begin your journey socializing with others over the Net, you might find yourself in the middle of an email or chat room conversation that you thought was going really well when the other party goes AWOL. That's the dabbler either getting bored or realizing that connection with another individual is not really what he or she is after.

The Nester

The Nester wants to find a committed relationship and is looking to the Internet as one of many ways to find one. He or she is usually very goal-oriented in that the purpose of socializing online is not about the process of forging friendships, but is about finding THE ONE PERSON that will be his or her lifetime mate.

The Hormone

The Hormone wants sex. Usually he or she will make this very clear early on. Hormones vary in that some just want virtual sex (that is, simulating sex via a private chat room discussion or email), some want to meet you in the physical world, and some want it in all manner, shape, and form.

The Butterfly

The Butterfly goes from chat room to chat room, person to person, having conversations with a multitude of different people. He or she is looking to make one or more friends and usually keep the relationship platonic. In a simpler time, this person went by the name penpal.

The Seeker

The Seeker doesn't know what he or she is looking for, but unlike the Dabbler, is seeking to make some sort of connection with another person. He or she might claim to be looking for a partner or just looking for sex, but the actual agenda is usually unknown to the Seeker.

Most people are obviously combinations of the different categories. One might be a Dabbler who dabbles at being a Hormone. Or a Seeker might find his true love and turn into a Nester. The important point to keep in mind is that even though there might be people on the Internet who share your interests, you want to also find the people who are looking for the same interpersonal goals that you are.

Know Thyself

Psychologists have been classifying individuals into different personality types for decades in the hopes of clarifying for people who they are and what they are seeking. If you'd like to learn more about your personality type in preparation for meeting people online, point your browser to `http://people.whitman.edu/~peterscc/psych/jung.html` and take the test provided. After you have the results, you'll need to surf over to `http://www.cs.colostate.edu/~pyeatt/myers-briggs.html` to interpret them.

What About All the Internet Nightmare Stories I've Heard About?

Are there dangerous people on the Internet?

Yes.

Do people online lie?

Some do.

Is it true that 60 percent of the Internet population consists of extra-terrestrials hell bent on taking over the planet?

If I answered that I'd have to take you up to the mother ship and dissect you.

Let's face it, the people on the Internet are the same people trying to meet you in the real world. The good, the bad, and the disenfranchised are all represented. If you protect yourself (see Chapter 3, "Was George Orwell Paranoid or an Optimist?"), your element of risk will be about the same as anywhere else.

The Least You Need to Know

➤ Everybody is afraid of getting hurt, especially people looking to meet others on the Net.

➤ Online socializing has been going on since the advent of the Internet in 1969.

➤ The Internet provides forums for meeting people based on very specific criteria such as Jewish vegetarians wanting to meet other Jewish vegetarians.

➤ Do not confuse a person's lifestyle or activity choices with what their interpersonal agenda might be.

➤ The people looking to meet you online are the same people looking to meet you in the real world.

Chapter 2

My Modem Blinks at Me and I Get Excited

In This Chapter

➤ What hardware do I need to socialize online?

➤ Why is my Internet connection sometimes slow?

➤ What kinds of software programs will we use to socialize online?

Let's face it: You're reading this book because you want to use your computer for the very human purpose of meeting other humans, not to listen to gobs of geek speak. As such, the section of this chapter dealing with the hardware requirements for online socializing could be boring and dry. To avoid this, *The Complete Idiot's Guide* is presenting this information in a form that has been successful with many other books containing hard to comprehend subject matter: as a conversation between the book's author and God. In this conversation, I will play the part of the author (someone knowledgeable about the online world) and Peter O'Toole will play the role of God (a being who knows nothing about computers).

Higher Power Concerns About Hardware

God: My dear lad, sit down. I have so many questions about computers and getting online.

Complete Idiot's Guide: But you're God. Shouldn't you know this stuff?

God: Dear, dear boy. Even God is confused by these things. So what kind of computer do I need to do all this online lallygagging?

CIG: Well, any of the activities we discuss in this book can be handled by most computers equipped with a modem and manufactured from 1997 to the present.

God: I have a note here from your editor asking you to go into more detail.

CIG: Why is God taking notes from my editor?

God: Why don't you just take a deep breath, have a biscuit, and have at it?

CIG: Okay. The actual computer you use doesn't much matter. If you want to use a Macintosh, an Imac or G3 (the two most popular Macs, as of this writing) will be more than serviceable. As for machines that run the various flavors of Windows, any Pentium-class computer (and that includes actual Pentium I, II, and IIIs as well as machines that utilize processors from other companies) with a speed of at least 133MHz (megahertz) will do just fine.

God: But what if I have an older computer?

CIG: Many older computers will work as well, but there are three factors that can affect online performance in computers old and new. They are your computer's video card, its modem, and your connection to the Internet.

God: Oh, I'm starting to miss my abacus!

CIG: Not to worry. Let's start with your computer's modem. Because the modem's job is to allow your computer to communicate with the Internet, the faster it is, the better. There's no reason to have a modem slower than 56kbps (kilobits per second), but faster modem technologies such as cable, DSL, and ISDN modems are not required for the online socializing we'll be exploring in this book.

God: Dear boy, I've used a 56K modem, but sometimes it seems like I'm waiting the length of a plague of locusts for a Web site to come up on my screen.

CIG: That could be because of your video card (sometimes referred to as the display adapter) or the quality of your Internet connection. The video card is important because information from the Web in the form of graphics and photographs can often seem to slow down your Web connection if you have to wait for your computer to draw the images on your screen. As a general rule of thumb, if your video card has at least 2 megabytes (MB) of memory (often denoted as VRAM for Video Random Access Memory or DRAM for Dynamic Random Access Memory), then you're probably okay to do most of the things we discuss in this book.

God: That seems rather simplified.

CIG: Well, it is. There's a whole lot more to video cards including the way they're configured and the amount of detail (resolution) you want to display. However, if your computer was manufactured in 1997 or later, you're probably okay.

God: Fiddlesticks! I lost my Internet connection. And I was half way to downloading the King James version of my book.

Figure 2.1

Even a deity will see this message if his Internet connection isn't divine.

CIG: People, and I mean no insult by including you in this group, sometimes become disconnected from the Internet or have slow connection speeds because the physical telephone wiring in their homes has lost some of its conductivity due to old age. As a result, the phone line can't carry as much information. Fortunately, this usually only affects wiring that is decades old or has been subjected to harsh conditions.

God: Speaking of harsh conditions, I told Richard Harris I'd go meet him at the pub.

In a moment of pique, I rip the halo off the bright light that stands in for the head of God. The light fades and I am confronted by a not so common man.

CIG: You're not God! You're Peter O'Toole.

Peter O'Toole: You've unmasked me.

CIG: Why the charade?

POT: Some will say it was vanity. Others will say it was just because you were desperate to fill pages as you were writing this book. But the real reason was that I am alone. And I thought if I could learn to use the Internet to meet people, I could somehow ease my pain.

CIG: You could read the rest of the book.

POT: No, dear boy. I can only wash my pain in the sands of the desert.

Figure 2.2

The PC Guide at `http://www.pcguide. com/ref/index.htm` *is an excellent resource for those who'd like to learn more about personal computing hardware.*

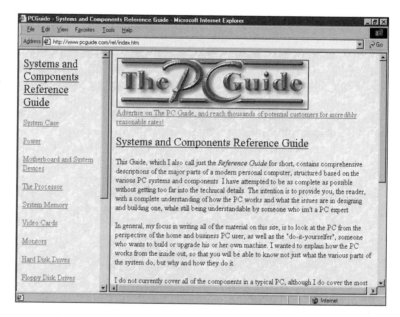

Peter O'Toole disappears. In his place is left a piece of paper with the Web address `http://www.pcguide.com/ref/index.htm`. I recognize it as the address of *The PC Guide,* an online resource that clearly explains the basics of personal computer hardware for those who want more detailed information.

Although his poor soul is left in wretched torment, I can only hope others will read on and discover the tools needed to find people compatible with themselves online. The quest continues with the proper software.

Don't I Already Have the Software I Need?

You need only three types of programs to socialize online. Fortunately, your computer might already have one or more of them installed. They are

➤ A Web browser

➤ An email program

➤ An instant messaging program

In addition, two other types of programs have been used traditionally to socialize online: chat programs and newsgroup readers. These days, however, Web browsers perform many of these programs' functions. As such, newcomers to online socializing can interact with others over the Internet without knowing much more than how to surf the Web. Those of you who will primarily be using a Web browser to socialize online can skip the rest of this chapter and go on to Chapter 3, "Was George Orwell Paranoid or an Optimist?" However, for those of you who would like a brief introduction to the five types of software just mentioned, let's begin by exploring the Web browser.

Blatant Plug

If you would like to know more about the inner workings of your computer, check out Ron White's book, *How Computers Work*, published by the same fine people who have brought to press the book you are now reading.

Web Browsers

A Web browser enables you to visit Web sites via your Internet connection. All new Windows and Macintosh computers come with Web browsers (and usually email programs and news readers as well), but for those who have older machines, are missing software, or just want to try a different program, here are the URLs (uniform resource locators)—or Web addresses—for Microsoft Internet Explorer and Netscape Communicator, the two most popular Web browsers:

Microsoft Internet Explorer for Windows

http://www.microsoft.com/windows/ie/download

Microsoft Internet Explorer for Macintosh

http://www.microsoft.com/mac/ie

Netscape Communicator for Windows or Macintosh

http://home.netscape.com/computing/download

The previous addresses will not only lead you to links for the most current browsers, but also to older browsers that are compatible with older equipment (see Figure 2.3).

Figure 2.3

Just type in the Web site's location in the address line, hit the Enter key, and you're on your way to surfing the Web.

On the Case

Although many Web addresses are case-insensitive, some, such as http://www.cnet.com/Help, are more finicky and require that certain letters be capitalized. Please note when uppercase is used within the Web addresses cited in this book.

After you are connected to the Internet, using a browser is a simple matter of typing the Web address you want to visit and pressing the **Enter** key. If you'd like to learn more about using Microsoft Internet Explorer or Netscape Communicator, press the **F1** key while in either program to explore help files for each browser or visit http://www.cnet.com/Help and click the link entitled **Internet** for some online tutorials.

Email Programs

Email allows you to send text messages to the millions of people on the Internet who also use email. The links in the Web browsers section of this chapter will allow you to download Outlook Express, Microsoft's email program that is often used with Internet Explorer, or Netscape Mail, which comes with Communicator. Once again, the **F1** key in either program will bring up the help system.

For those who would like another email alternative, Qualcomm manufactures a third free email program entitled Eudora Light. It can be downloaded at http://eudora.qualcomm.com/eudoralight. One of the Web's first email programs, Eudora Light, is used by tens of millions of people and comes with a manual you can download from the same Web page.

Instant Messaging Programs

Instant messaging programs allow you to maintain a list of the people you regularly socialize with online, notifying you when those on your list are connected to the Internet. You can then send them messages that they get immediately (without recipients having to retrieve them as in many email packages), start a chat session, send files (including pictures), and a host of other activities. Unfortunately, the people you keep in contact with must be using the same software that you're using. In Chapter 11, "The Velvet Rope," we will explore instant messaging's many capabilities using a variety of software packages, including two of the most popular ones: ICQ and AOL Instant Messenger.

The Gift That Keeps on Giving

One method of online communication not covered in this book is the Internet mailing list, otherwise known as a listserv. These mailing lists, which are designed to disseminate information on a single topic via email, come in two varieties: moderated and unmoderated. Both types basically work the same: When you have some discussion point to make, you send it off in an email to a central address. In a moderated mailing list, someone culls through the emails and then condenses the ones he or she chooses into a single correspondence sent at regular intervals (for example, once a week) to all the list's subscribers. But in an unmoderated mailing list, each email sent to the central address is automatically forwarded to every person who has subscribed to the list. This can result in list members receiving dozens of emails each day. Because most Internet mailing lists are unmoderated, you should make sure you know how to remove yourself from any list before you subscribe to it (most mailing lists post instructions for unsubscribing at the time and place you subscribe). In this way, you'll be able to stop receiving listserv emails should the volume or topic matter be unwanted. Most mailing lists will continue to send you email until you unsubscribe or cancel your email account.

Newsgroup Readers

There is a part of the Internet called Usenet that is basically the equivalent of the cork bulletin board at the local laundromat. Anyone with a newsgroup reader can post messages on Usenet for the entire Internet community to read, as well as read all the messages posted by others. So unlike email, which is addressed to specific individuals, newsgroup readers post messages for the entire world to see.

Because Usenet must deal with millions of messages each year, it is divided into newsgroups, each an individual posting area devoted to a specific topic. There are thousands of newsgroups with topics ranging from the highly technical to the highly personal, but those who are offended by salty language must tread lightly in parts of Usenet because it is mostly an uncensored environment.

Although this book will explore Web sites that allow you to access Usenet newsgroups with your Web browser, Microsoft provides a newsgroup reader as part of Outlook Express and Netscape has its own newsgroup reader that is part of Communicator. For those who would like to explore other newsgroup readers, there are dozens of other choices. Most can be downloaded from `http://www.download.com`. Click the link entitled **Internet** followed by the **Newsreaders** link and sample the buffet.

Because of the popularity of Usenet Newsgroups, the World Wide Web has expanded to include Web-based message boards. Web-based message boards are used in exactly the same way as Usenet Newsgroups. The only difference is that you must use a Web browser to access a Web-based message board because newsreader software is unable to read information posted on a Web page.

Chat Programs

Chat programs allow you to talk to people (well, actually type messages) and receive replies immediately as if you were having a conversation in the same room. Although most of the chatting discussed in this book will simply use a Web browser, there are at least a dozen other software programs that allow you to chat online. We will discuss chatting using a Web browser, as well as some of these other chatting environments, in Chapter 10, "Why Is Everyone Talking About Medieval Cookware?"

The Least You Need to Know

➤ If your computer was manufactured in 1997 or later, you probably have the hardware you need to socialize online.

➤ A 56K modem is more than adequate for socializing online. Although faster technologies like cable modems are nice, they are not necessary for what we will be learning about in this book.

➤ Many Windows and Apple computers come with much of the software you need for online socializing including a Web browser, email program, and newsgroup reader. Some also come with chat and instant messaging software.

Chapter 3

Was George Orwell Paranoid or an Optimist?

> ### In This Chapter
>
> ➤ Learn how to keep yourself safe while socializing online
>
> ➤ Discover how to guard your anonymity
>
> ➤ Explore organizations devoted to interpersonal online safety

In simpler days, a stalker might have been someone who could husk a lot of corn, but now, unfortunately, that word has a more sinister meaning. So do words like pervert, molester, deviant, rapist, murderer, and scuzbag, all of which could make anyone stop socializing beyond their known circle of friends. Add to the known dangers of dating and relating the fact that you are doing this in cyberspace, and some people become terrified. However, the miscreants of the Internet are actually a very small percentage of the online community and if you follow some simple precautions, dating and relating online can be as safe, if not safer, than the tried and true happenstance that the physical world embraces.

Guidelines for Keeping Yourself Safe

There are two important components to keeping yourself safe while exploring the online interpersonal waters: factors controlled by you and those controlled by technology. Let's start with you.

Take Your Time

You meet someone in a chat room or via an online personal ad and the two of you immediately gel. Similar values, likes and dislikes combined with a growing feeling that this person "understands me" urge you towards giving out your phone number or arranging to meet in person. But should you? Not if you feel rushed. Many times because of loneliness, sexual desire, or desperation we might go against our better judgement and jump headlong into a relationship using a rationalization along the lines of "you've got to take risks to succeed." But the difference between risk-taking and foolishness is taking the time to think. Do you feel you've spent enough time online with this person? Have there been any major red flags (see later in this chapter)? Has this person answered all your questions to your satisfaction? If you feel the time is right to move the relationship along, go for it. If the other person wants to go to another level and you're not ready, ask for more time to get to know her or him better online. If he or she starts pressuring you, it's time for you to explain to this person that you'll only do things when you're ready or, better still, move on to someone else.

Be Inquisitive

In relating, as in third grade, there are no stupid questions. Early on in my own online dating adventures, I met a woman who seemed like great fun. We shared many interests and she was quite a lovely writer. Still I had the feeling something was not quite right. So I decided to ask her if she was married. I never heard from her again. The point of this morality tale is that there are two types of liars: those who lie outright and those who conceal via omission. Asking questions will not weed out the out-right liars, but will often save you from dealing with many who would otherwise deceive through a convenient silence.

Watch for Red Flags

There are a few simple warning signs, or red flags, to watch for when socializing online.

Vagueness or Nonresponsiveness

When conversing with someone online, are they being vague or ignoring your questions altogether? With an email relationship, your correspondent might simply have forgotten to answer your query, but if you ask the same question several times and haven't received a valid response, the person to whom you're writing might be hiding something. Remember, there is a difference between a person not wanting to give out a home address and when asked what he or she does for a living responds, "You know. Stuff."

Disappearing

Some people you socialize with online might disappear for days or weeks at a time. As always, circumstances play a great deal in determining whether this is a red flag or not. If the person informs you that he or she will be out of touch before disappearing and if it happens only once, then there's probably no cause for concern. However, if a pattern of being out of communication for days or weeks at a time develops, this person could have an agenda that conflicts with yours.

Availability Only at Odd Hours

Different people have different lifestyles. If a person can't go online evenings or weekends, it might mean he or she has no computer at home, and must socialize from the office. Then again, this person could be concealing his or her Internet activity from a spouse or lover. As such, you might want to get into the habit of checking the time stamp on emails you receive from your online correspondents. If they are consistently writing you at 3 a.m., you should ask why. The answer might be that your email pal works nights, or it might be that "3 a.m. is the only time I can sneak into the prison library to use the computer."

Internet Harassment

Internet harassment is very rare, but unfortunately it does happen. Just as you would report an obscene phone caller to the authorities, you should also report those who would threaten or harass you via email, instant messaging, or any other online communication. If you are harassed via email or instant messaging, notify your Internet service provider and, if you feel the possibility of physical danger exists, the police. Make sure to save any written communications sent to you, as these messages can be used to track down the offender. If you are being harassed on a Web-based chat room, contact the owners of the Web site. In addition, do not hesitate to contact CyberAngels (discussed later in this chapter), an organization dedicated to online interpersonal safety.

Quick Emotional Attachment

As you might have heard from newspaper articles or television shows, it is very easy for some people to get emotionally involved just by revealing their deepest feelings over a modem. Well, as the poet says, mature love takes time to grow. You might want to question the longevity of someone's emotions if they claim to love you or feel delirious about you after a few chat sessions or emails. And if you start developing what seems to be deep feelings of love for someone online after only a short time, you might want to ask yourself, "How well do I really know this person?"

Spelling and History Counts Sometimes

When I was a child, there were other kids in the neighborhood who liked to make prank phone calls (of course, I never participated, instead preferring to spend my time honing my dating skills). These were harmless jests, which, at most, caused the occasional butcher to wonder how he could walk if he had pig's feet. These days, however, many teens have computers and some of them like to toy with the opposite, and sometimes same, sex. I know of a few stories in which an obvious lack of knowledge about basic spelling and current or historical events has unmasked an online socializer as someone pretending to be five to twenty years older than he or she actually is. Of course, this could also mean that the person you are conversing with online is just a lousy speller who gets depressed by the news.

Only Give Sensitive Information Sparingly and When You're Ready

Many online relationships that move into the offline world follow this progression:

1. Meet online, usually anonymously.
2. Exchange email or instant messaging addresses and continue the online relationship via chat, written correspondence, or both.
3. Progress to a phone relationship.
4. Meet in the physical world.

In each of the previous stages, you will have to relinquish some private information and, as always, should do so only when you feel comfortable. However, there are other pieces of personal information you should be careful with:

➤ The first thing many people will want to know is your name, because you'll probably only be known at first via an anonymous pseudonym (usually referred to as a handle). Revealing a first name after a couple of emails or when chatting in private with another is not a huge problem for some, but if your name is unusual or you are not comfortable in any way, continue to use your pseudonym. Under no circumstances should you reveal your last name until you feel very comfortable with someone. Even if this means months of online socializing with this person before you're sure.

➤ When you discuss where you live, do not give out your home address. Instead, give the general location. People who live in a well-populated urban area could mention the neighborhood they live in without being identified, but people who reside in sparsely populated areas should probably just mention the county they live in or a city they live near.

➤ Be careful when discussing your job. If you live in a big city, for example, mentioning that you're an insurance adjuster reveals little about who you work for. However, if you're in an area where a top insurance company has its corporate headquarters and there's not much else for 50 miles, you might unwittingly give someone your work address.

➤ Do not reveal your social security number or any financial or credit card information. If someone asks for these things, you should cease contact with that person.

Enter the Offline World Cautiously

Entering the physical world begins not with a face-to-face meeting, but with revealing your phone number. Never reveal your home phone number until you are comfortable with doing so. If you'd like to talk to someone you've met online, but don't feel safe enough to give out your number, get his or her number and initiate the call yourself from a phone that will not compromise your privacy via Caller ID (a service that reveals the caller's telephone number to the person being called). The only problem is if neither of you want to give out a home telephone number, you will have to work out some combination of using beepers, call-forwarding, or pay phones to converse by phone.

If, after talking on the phone, you decide you want to meet this person face to face, here are some guidelines to consider for your first meeting:

➤ Meet in a well-traveled public place during the day. It never hurts to be around others while you assess how safe you feel. And having your own transportation is also great should you feel the need for a quick exit.

➤ Tell someone you trust about the date (including details of where, when, and with whom) before you go on it. You can even arrange to call this person to "check in" during the date. That way, in a worst case scenario, someone can call for help even if you can't.

➤ If you own a cellular phone, charge it fully and keep it on your person during the date. These devices are obviously useful in all sorts of stressful situations.

Use Your Instincts

Notice that the previous headline does not say "Trust Your Instincts." Let's face it: There are some people who occasionally or consistently make poor choices when picking prospective dating partners. If you are one of those, you should exercise additional caution above and beyond this chapter's advice. If someone cares about meeting and getting to know you, he or she will understand your cautious behavior.

If you are one of those people who generally have good instincts, then by all means do trust them. Remember, if something feels wrong, it's not worth your personal safety to ignore it. Err on the side of caution.

Keeping Your Identity Anonymous

Now that you're practicing safe online socializing, it's time to make sure your computer is as well. Many people who give away their identity unwillingly do so because of the technology they are using. Here are some things to watch for:

➤ Almost every program, whether it is of the chat, email, newsgroup, or instant messaging variety, has a preferences or personal information section that reveals information about the user. Sometimes this information was put in when the program was installed or, if you're computing in a corporate setting, is generated automatically with each use. To maintain anonymity, make sure you check the preferences and operating options for each program you're using to control what information it gives out.

➤ Many programs append signatures to their communications. A signature is an addendum placed on the end of an email, chat communication, newsgroup posting, or instant message. In a corporate environment, this often can contain specifics such as your name, work address, and work telephone number.

➤ Email programs are particularly guilty of the previous. As discussed later in this chapter, if you have any doubts about the information your email program is revealing, I strongly suggest using Web-based email. In any event, always send yourself an email from your own account before you start corresponding with strangers. At least you'll have a preview of what your email program is sending out to others.

➤ Be very wary of using software on your work computer (especially if you're in a corporate environment) for online socializing. Although you might take the previous precautions and disable all processes for revealing your identity, a network technician or other information systems person could unwittingly restore your information while servicing your machine. Again, when in doubt, use Web-based technologies.

Web-Based Email

One of the best tools for maintaining online anonymity is Web-based email. There are literally hundreds of Web sites that offer free email to anyone with Internet access, usually in exchange for viewing an advertising banner that is displayed with each new Web page. Although these Web services usually require that a first and last name be sent out with each email, this hurdle to anonymity is easily gotten around. One national Web-based email service I've found to be excellent is Yahoo! Mail found at `http://mail.yahoo.com` (see Figure 3.1).

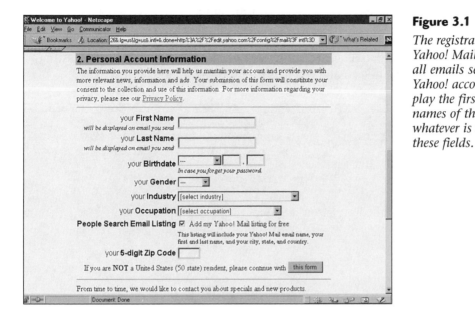

Figure 3.1

The registration form for Yahoo! Mail. Note that all emails sent from a Yahoo! account will display the first and last names of the sender or whatever is typed into these fields.

Whenever you sign up for free Web-based email, there will almost always be a Terms of Service (TOS) Agreement or similar legal contract that you will have to agree to in order to use the service. Although many people never read these agreements, you should note that there is almost always a clause like this one from the Yahoo! Mail TOS:

> "You agree to provide true and correct information about yourself in the Yahoo! Mail Terms of Service registration form."

Now, I think our parents all made it very clear that one should never lie. But when you fill out your first and last names when registering for your free email account, who is to say you are known by your birth name. Many of us go by fanciful nicknames like Snagglepuss or Smiley Face. Or, coincidentally, by whatever handle the email account has (for example, your email account might be RockCollector@yahoo.com and you go by the name "Rock Collector.") Or even your initials. As long as you are not going to defraud another or participate in illegal activities, you should put whatever first and last name is "true and correct" about yourself, but still provides you with the safety that you need to socialize online. It should also be noted that after your email account is established, many free Web-based email services, including Yahoo! Mail, allow you to change the first and last names the account generates when it sends out emails.

Other free email services include Microsoft's Hotmail found at `http://www.hotmail.com` and Netscape WebMail located at `http://webmail.netscape.com`. If you'd like to see the full tapestry of free email services on the Web, point your browser to `http://www.emailaddresses.com` (see Figure 3.2). There you'll find a comprehensive listing containing most of the free email providers on the Web.

Figure 3.2

The Free Email Address Directory at www.emailaddresses.com has links to hundreds of free Web-based email services.

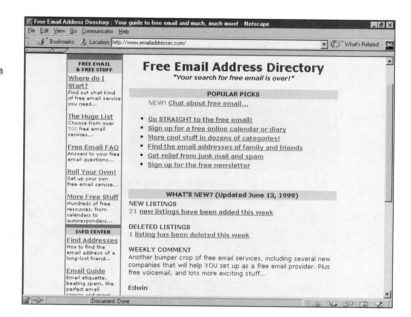

Personal Ad Services and Anonymous Remailers

If you're thinking of exploring the world of online personal ads, there is one more safety tool you should know about. Some of the more established services use anonymous remailers, which are basically computer programs that intercept your email, strip out your original address, and then replace the deleted information with an anonymous handle before sending it onto its final destination. In this way, the recipient never has access to your actual email address. Many people who date online seek this feature out for the extra safety it provides. Be aware though, that if you use these services (offered by some of the Web sites in Chapter 5, "Do You Type Here Often?" and Chapter 6, "I Want Values for My Money"), you'll still have to maintain the safety steps discussed earlier. Even though an anonymous remailer will strip out your address in the "To:" part of an email, it will not remove references to your address in the body of the correspondence or appended signatures.

Using the Web to Protect Yourself

Not surprisingly, there are a number of Web sites devoted to keeping you safe as you start interacting with those you meet online in both the online and offline worlds.

SmartDate

http://www.smartdate.com

The concept behind SmartDate (see Figure 3.3) is simple: For $12/year (as of this writing) each member receives an online diary for the purpose of recording all dating plans in advance of actually going on each date. The idea is that in a worse-case scenario, should you disappear, local law enforcement officials can gain access to your diary and learn what your whereabouts were prior to whatever trouble has befallen you. The diary can also be used to document travel plans, sexual harassment, or any event you feel might be threatening or potentially dangerous. Unlike a diary you keep in your home (which might take precious time to locate in an emergency), if friends and relatives know you are using the SmartDate Web site to record your social plans, law-enforcement authorities can gain access to your writings upon the filing of a missing persons report.

Figure 3.3

Law enforcement officials can access your SmartDate diary and find out your whereabouts and any dating particulars you've recorded should your date end disastrously.

CyberAngels

http://www.cyberangels.org

CyberAngels, which bills itself as the largest online Internet safety program since 1995, is an organization best known for their Net Patrol, an online neighborhood watch that monitors cyberspace for child pornographers and predators. However, they also help people who are harassed and stalked online by assisting them in identifying and reporting offenders to the proper authorities. Hopefully it's a site you'll never have to visit, but if you have gotten yourself into a situation where someone online will not leave you alone, they have a wide range of resources and information.

Personal Safety for Women

Although dating online and off can be fraught for both sexes, women must be especially careful not to enter into situations where they can be put in physical danger. One organization, AWARE (Arming Women Against Rape and Endangerment), has a Web site (http://www.aware.org) that addresses this concern. It contains a great deal of information on the topic of personal safety, including a lengthy section answering questions about self-defense and the prevention of hazardous situations. AWARE provides a great resource for women who want to learn more about keeping themselves physically safe in interpersonal encounters.

DateSmart.com

http://datesmart.com

Not to be confused with the aforementioned SmartDate, DateSmart is a company devoted to providing confidential background checks for people in personal relationships. For example, if you're getting involved with someone you met online (or otherwise) and you have reason to be suspicious, you can spend (as of this writing) $95-$145 for a basic background check that will provide name verification to confirm if they are who they say they are; search for felony or misdemeanor criminal records; list any civil filings (bankruptcy, tax liens, and so on) they've made; and delve into your amour's history and records with the department of motor vehicles (alcohol or drug arrests, failure to pay fines, and so on). Should you want additional checks done, such as marital status or prison record, they will provide those for an additional fee.

Check-A-Date

`http://www.check-a-date.com`

Check-A-Date provides a service somewhat identical to DateSmart, but its basic background check (or personal profiler/background ID as they call it) costs (as of this writing) $79.95 and provides slightly different information. (For example, criminal records are not included, but you will find out whether your prospective owns an air or watercraft).

The Least You Need to Know

➤ Though it can be easy to be swept up in a cyber–romance, always take your time when meeting someone new and keep safety as your first concern.

➤ When socializing online with new people, be careful to note possible red flags such as vagueness, nonresponsiveness, and their lack of availability evenings and weekends.

➤ Check to make sure that the computer programs you use do not give away personal information accidentally.

➤ Be very careful what personal information you give out and to whom you give it. Some information, such as credit card and social security numbers, should never be divulged.

➤ Exercise caution when meeting an online acquaintance for the first time in the offline world. Do not hesitate to make sure others know where and when this meeting takes place and arrange for a check-in call during your first encounter.

➤ Be aware that there are online organizations devoted to helping you remain safe while you meet people online.

Part 2
Dating Bytes

This part of the book is for those looking to go on dates with the people they meet online. We'll begin by exploring how to write an online personal ad; how to prepare a picture for posting with your ad or exchanging with those you meet; and how to communicate using the abbreviations and symbols common to online interaction. Next, we'll take a tour of more than two dozen personal ad Web sites, many of which cater to specific communities based on age, religion, sexual preference, or other criteria. After you meet a person who interests you, the chapter on Web sites designed to help you romance someone online will come in handy. And finally, should you feel the need for romantic advice, we have a chapter that guides you toward those who will provide real guidance and others who will just try to make you laugh.

Chapter 4

Is That Email in Your Inbox, or Are You Just Happy to Read Me?

In This Chapter

➤ What to do and avoid doing when writing your online personal ad

➤ Tips for preparing a photograph should you want to let someone you meet online know what you look like

➤ Cyber-flirting suggestions

➤ A personal recollection about an online relationship

What is dating? An obvious answer might be to get acquainted with one person or many people over the course of multiple interactions with the goal of finding a mate. But anyone who's been out there knows that depending on the individual, dating can mean the search for sex, an activity partner, a caretaker, a confidante, someone to experiment with, or any combination of these and others. The good news is that whatever you're looking for, there's a place on the Internet to find it, and a Web-based personal ad is a great way to start. In Chapter 5, "Do You Type Here Often?" and Chapter 6, "I Want Values for My Money," we'll tour the actual Web sites for placing your ad, but first let's explore writing one.

Getting Personal with Personal Ads

The biggest mistake people make when writing their personal ads is creating one while they are online at the Web site they plan to list it on. A cursory exploration of the online ad terrain will display oodles of ads that begin with variations on "I really don't know what to say" and "I'm not used to writing about myself." I suggest you read through the tips that follow, type up your ad in advance on your word processor, and then when you place your ad, copy the text onto the Web site's registration form.

Choose an Identity Carefully

Almost every Web site that lists personals will require you to use a handle or alias so you can receive emails from interested parties without revealing your name. The choice of what your pseudonym will be is a key decision for your personal ad as it is usually the first thing your prospective respondents will see and will announce a great deal about your personality or desires. Here are some tips to choosing your perfect handle:

Make It Meaningful

It is always amazing to me how often a person's handle will be something generic like "Girl1024" or "WorkingGuy34." Not only do these examples tell very little about the writer other than gender (and in WorkingGuy's case, that he might not have a lot of time to spare), but the number usually suggests that there is nothing particularly special about the writer because there are dozens of others using an almost identical handle.

One way to give your handle meaning is to make an easily recognizable connection to some activity or pursuit you participate in. For example, TennisFiend, clearly likes to volley and serve while BronteLover has an affinity for Charlotte, Emily, and Anne Bronte, three sisters who wrote poetry and prose in the 1800s. What's particularly nice about using this method is that you not only announce a life passion, but you also dissuade people who do not share your interest from contacting you. Of course you should only use this method for creating a handle if you have a true passion for something.

Another way to make it meaningful is to create a handle that contains a slightly obscure reference or inside joke. For example, FeathersMcGraw could be a handle for someone who loves the Wallace and Gromit animated films. People who've seen "The Wrong Trousers," the film in which this character appears, would get the reference immediately, while others might read the personal ad just based on the handle's novelty. A side benefit to choosing a handle this way is that it can often start a conversation when people ask you what your handle refers to.

Be Descriptive

There's no doubt that men and women can be visually stimulated. A good descriptive handle can start that process even before Web surfers gaze upon your countenance. PerkyBlonde or MarlboroMan tell us that the former is probably a woman (men don't often describe themselves as perky) who is an energetic and fun-loving blonde. The latter is a guy's guy: rugged, individualistic, and solid. Be aware though that depending on what associations come to the mind of the reader, your descriptive ad might be taken the wrong way. The PerkyBlonde could be thought of as annoying, while the MarlboroMan might be mistaken for a heavy smoker. Fortunately, you can always explain your handle further in the actual personal ad.

Be Suggestive

The difference between a handle that's descriptive and one that's suggestive is the descriptive ad says something about the way you look, act, or run your life, while the suggestive one implies a goal or course of action. HoldMyHand is a handle that might suggest this person is looking for affection and companionship while WildRide might be implying the need for a more physically active relationship. If you decide to use a suggestive handle, and especially if you don't, be careful that you don't unintentionally create a double entendre.

Create an Attention-Grabbing Headline

Many personal ad sites require you to compose a headline for your ad. This is important not only as an introduction to the ad itself, but because many sites initially provide surfers with only a list of ad headlines. If someone likes your headline, he or she might then click a link and view your entire ad.

Just as you might do for your handle, you can use your headline to describe yourself or what you're looking for. Most probably though, the personal ad Web site has a search function that guides the person looking at your headline to see a list of headlines based on gender, age, geographic location, and a host of other factors. As such, you could also use your headline to draw attention to your ad by amplifying some aspect of your personality or by just being playful. Here are some examples of headlines that fall into this category:

"Yes, I'd Love Some Wine. Thank You."

"The Store Shelves Are All Empty. Wait, There's One Left!"

"She Looked Like Trouble. Well, Maybe That's What I Was in the Market For."

"Get me some Cheezipoofs!"

"Pick Me! Pick Me!"

Honestly Describe Yourself and What You're Looking For

There is no greater letdown than meeting face to face with someone you've interacted with online and finding out that he or she was less than truthful in describing his or her appearance. The same is true when you find out your date who professed a love for all your passions really just wanted to sound accommodating. Though we always want to show ourselves in a positive light, it is essential that your ad is truthful. Don't, for instance, say you're muscular when you're actually slight of build. Not everyone wants a bodybuilder, and people are always happier when they feel they've been dealt with honestly.

This rule becomes doubly important when you're writing what you want in regards to a relationship and the person you're looking for. For instance, if you're just looking for sex, you should say so to attract people with a similar goal. This doesn't mean you have to write "I only want sexual relationships" (although there's nothing wrong with this), but it does mean being clear in your goals. If someone who only wants sex states something to the effect "I'm only looking for short-term relationships and to have some fun," this at least tells those people who are looking for committed relationships to move on.

Reveal Something About Yourself

When people create their personal ads, they usually list activities and pursuits that they are involved in. There is definitely a place for some of this information in your ad, but a laundry list of things you do does not necessarily make you or your ad interesting. Personal revelations concerning your life, how you feel about things, the way you think, and just quirky observations will reveal your personality and thus make the ad more representative of who you are. I'm not saying you should reveal deeply moving or traumatic events from your life, but you should try to differentiate yourself from the other ads by showing that there is a real person behind the writing. Some examples of personal revelations in online ads are:

"I like to walk on the beach. I feel at home near the water."

"Have you noticed how all the ATMs now charge you a buck or more if you don't have an account at that particular bank? Well I remember when it was free and if it bothers you as much as I, perhaps we should talk."

"Pancakes are a favorite food of mine. My mother used to make them for me as a child, and they're still my favorite comfort food."

"My friends say I'm too picky. Well, it's important to me to be picky when I'm looking for someone to spend my life with."

Create a Little Mystery

To paraphrase the old saw, a man or woman ceases to be interesting when all mystery is lost. So how do you cultivate mystery in a personal ad while still being open and forthright about your description, goals, and desires? One way is to reveal only part of a fact with the hope that learning the rest will peak someone's interest. For example, if you've traveled throughout Europe, you could state in your ad that you've "traveled extensively" (which would be too general), list every country you've been to, or say something like "I've visited the homes of five different European rulers." If someone who shares your interest in travel reads the latter, it might get them to write to you to find out what countries you've been to and to learn more about your adventurous spirit.

Another way to create mystery is to ask questions or pose a playful challenge. "Can anyone help me with this crossword? I need a five-letter word for pungent," would announce to the online personal ad community that you love crossword puzzles and are looking for someone to share this interest with. It also creates mystery for other crossword puzzle aficionados who can't figure out what the five-letter word is. (For those who can't stand a mystery, the answer I was looking for is "acrid.")

It is important to note that in both the previous stratagems, you do not want to deceive anyone, just pique their interest. And even more importantly, to pique the interest not of the general population, but of those who might be compatible with you.

Be Specific

I have a friend, who, for anonymity's sake, we'll call Henry. Henry is 5'9" in height. Henry considers himself tall. When he writes to women over the Internet, they are often upset to find out that he is not over 6' in height. Why? Because when they wrote their ad, they used a phrase similar to "Please be tall." Had they written "Please be over 6' tall," this hilarity could have been avoided.

The preceding illustrates a principle that you should use in all aspects of writing your ad: Be as specific as possible. Some of the better personal ad sites try to help you do this by requiring you to fill out a thumbnail description of what you're looking for, which is then posted with your ad.

Be Positive

It is almost impossible to peruse personal ads on Web sites without running into those that lay out the type of person not wanted. "If you are a loser, do not write me," is typical of these ads. Let's examine the word "loser." Now, you and I know who all the losers are, but I've rarely known a loser who admits to being one. In fact, many of the losers think that you and I are losers. So despite this admonition, many of the losers end up writing personal ads to those who would rather not be contacted by them.

A better way to approach your ad is to be positive and, again, specifically state what you do want in the person you are trying to meet. It is the difference between writing negatively, "No Smokers, please!" and stating positively "Please be a nonsmoker."

Common Personal Ad Pitfalls to Avoid

Now that we've discussed some of the ways to make your personal ad effective, let's quickly look at some pitfalls you should try to avoid while writing it.

Avoid the Laundry List

Although we are all complex human beings with wide and varied interests, there's no reason you need to put every one of them in your ad. Here's an excerpt from a typical laundry list ad:

> *"A little about me. I enjoy skiing, tennis, baseball, basketball, traveling (I've been to Europe twice!), my job, movies, good books, TV sitcoms, all types of music, spending time with my close friends and family, eating at new restaurants, comedy clubs, going to the theater (Broadway, off-Broadway, cabaret), singing, shopping, long walks on the beach, watching the sunset, talking about everything from art to politics, animals, volunteering, sailing, a night on the town, and quiet evenings at home."*

Now, I have no doubt this person does enjoy all these things, but there is no sense of who she is other than a busy person who likes everything life has to offer with the possible exception of breathing (and I'm only guessing that because it was one of the few things not on the list). I would suggest to this person that she pick the four or five activities that mean the most to her and briefly elaborate on them—because as we'll see in the next paragraph, the laundry list is the flipside of another pitfall.

Embody the Soul of Wit

My tenth-grade English teacher was fond of endlessly quoting Polonius' famous line from Shakespeare's *Hamlet*, "...brevity is the soul of wit." I'm willing to bet that she would have written a kick-ass personal ad. She knew that it's easy to lose your audience by listing dozens of pieces of minutia. Obviously, if your personal has very little or no information, it will probably not attract much, or the desired, attention, so it's important to strike a balance. Still, it's always good to keep in mind my teacher's other famous cliché, "less is more."

Act Upon Self-Subjectivity

I've heard personal ads described as "a form of bragging." But the fact is that only the poorly written personal ads are of a boastful and often empty nature, while the truthful ones are usually the most interesting. There is no better example of this than when someone tries to describe themselves objectively with subjective terms. "I've got a great sense of humor" is one of these phrases. But what does that mean? I probably laugh at different things than you, and both of us might find very unfunny what a third person laughs at uproariously. The point is, rather than just write "I've got a great sense of humor," actually display your sense of humor in the ad. Make a wry comment, tell a joke, or reference comedians you like. Other examples of this type of bragging include "I'm very successful," "Men find me attractive," and "I'm a normal person."

It's Raining Cats and Dogs on My Personal!

Although it has always been a mainstay of good writing to avoid clichés, the proliferation of personal ads has created a subset of clichés that are common to these ads. They include:

"I'll try anything once! Well almost anything."

"I'm comfortable in black tie or jeans."

"...a night on the town or quiet evenings at home."

"I'm a complete package."

Any reference to the words "soul mate."

Any reference to your mother.

As always, using a cliché will not make your ad an egregious eyesore, but the more you can avoid commonly used phrases, the more successful you'll be at differentiating your ad from the rest.

Be Confident

Dating books through the decades have extolled the virtues of confidence. The beauty of a personal ad is that you don't have to summon up the brave face you might require meeting someone in person. All you have to do is make sure you don't sound unsure in your ad. Phrases like "I'm not sure what I'm doing here" and "I really feel odd writing this" only detract from your ad. It is a given that most people would rather not have to advertise for their personal or romantic needs. However, if you sound like you're comfortable with the personal ad process, that will make you all the more attractive to others, even those who are unsure themselves. And after you start communicating with someone else, imagine how three-dimensional, not to mention human, you'll appear admitting that you are not totally at ease with the online personal ad process.

Use Capitalization Sparingly

No one likes to be screamed at, which is what typing in all caps represents on the Internet. Just as sentences written in all capital letters is considered offensive in emails and other online communications, the same is true for your personal ad. Also, it is often very hard to read ads written this way.

Reading and Replying to Other Ads

The last pitfall to avoid actually concerns responding to other people's ads. Many personals will contain specific requests for what the writer is looking for from others. Although you might have a strong wish for connecting with someone, you should always read other ads carefully and abide by the writer's wishes. For example, someone might be looking for a partner who practices a particular religion. Despite the fact that you believe you are a perfect match, unless you plan to also practice that religion, move on and do not respond to the ad.

How's Your Personal Ad Doing?

The lifespan of an online personal ad can vary, but on average, it will certainly be in circulation longer than those that would appear in a printed publication. As a result, you might want to revise your ad from time to time. Use this handy checklist to review what elements you want to keep or revise in a personal ad you've already written.

- ❏ Is my handle meaningful, descriptive, suggestive, or memorable in some way?
- ❏ Does my ad headline grab a person's attention?
- ❏ Do I describe myself honestly?
- ❏ Have I honestly related what I'm looking for?
- ❏ Have I revealed something of myself as a person?
- ❏ Did I create any mystery?
- ❏ Is the ad specific?
- ❏ Is the ad positive?
- ❏ Did I avoid making the ad into a laundry list?
- ❏ Is the ad filled with enough information to say what's important, but brief enough so that people aren't intimidated by its length?
- ❏ Did I avoid describing myself objectively with subjective terms (for example, "I have a great sense of humor")?
- ❏ Did I abstain from using clichés (especially those common to online personal ads)?
- ❏ Did I eschew sentences written entirely in capital letters?
- ❏ Is the tone of the ad confident?

If you need to review how to implement these concepts into your ad, they are all discussed in detail later in this chapter.

Photograph Yeas and Nays

Many of the online personal ad Web sites allow people to include photographs of themselves with their ad (see Figures 4.1 and 4.2). However, putting your face on the Internet for millions of people to see does compromise your anonymity. Again as with everything else we discuss in this book, only post a photograph with your ad if you're comfortable doing so. Some people believe that ads with photographs get more responses than those without, but a photograph does not ensure a good response to your personal, and many ads are successful without one.

Figure 4.1

Notice how little thought this man put into his appearance for this photo.

Figure 4.2

This second try presents the subject in a better light.

I recommend that those of you who will not be featuring your picture with your ad still get a photograph of yourself scanned (the process of taking a photo and converting it to a file so that your picture can be viewed on your computer). After you've been communicating with someone online for a while, you might want to exchange photos by sending them via email attachment. Even if you do not own a scanner, many copy shops, especially those that belong to national chains, will scan your photo and place it on a floppy disk for a small fee. If you go this route, request that the photo be scanned in as a .jpg (pronounced jay-peg) image. All Windows and Macintosh computers can read this type of file using a Web browser or other software. After you have the file you can copy it onto your computer at home.

If you decide to prepare a photograph for your personal ad and/or to share with new online acquaintances, keep in mind that you want the photo to look like you so that people who meet you after seeing it don't feel like you've tried to deceive them. Don't use pictures that are several years old, retouched, or only show part of your face. Also make sure that the photo is of good quality, neither over- or under-exposed. This is especially important because, depending on the skill of the person who prepares the electronic copy of your photo, you might lose some quality in the scanning process.

You also might want to pay some attention to what's going on in the photograph. There seems to be a whole cabal of people who post photographs of themselves with the disembodied arm of their previous boyfriend or girlfriend draped around their shoulder or waist. Now I'm not saying there's anything wrong with cutting off the half of the photo with your ex, but whenever I see one of those pictures I inevitably think "What's the story there?"

Finally, when viewing the photos of people you're interested in, it's important to remember that photographs can often be inexact in their representation of others. Not only do the things to watch for when preparing your own photograph apply, but some people are simply not photogenic and meeting them in person will often be very different from any picture they could supply.

Kodak Questions

Often the simple act of seeing someone's photo via email attachment, Web page, instant messaging, or some other means can raise questions. Do not hesitate to ask your correspondent about the photo you've seen, as long as you do so positively. There is a huge difference between writing "It seems like you sent me a five-year-old picture" and "I noticed the banner in your photo said '1995 Fundraiser.' I'm guessing you still look pretty much the same today."

The Direct Approach

In recent years, some people have built their own Web sites and devoted them to finding a compatible other (see Figure 4.3). On the plus side, this direct approach allows anyone with an Internet connection to find you, not just the people who have signed up with a personal ads site. On the negative side, all anonymity is lost, and you have to confront the work involved in promoting your Web address and registering your site with search engines so that people will stumble upon your page (although some have helped this process along by providing a link to their Web page within a personal ad). I think it's probably more effective and safe to go with an established personal ads site that offers anonymity and other services, but the direct approach is definitely being tried by some very brave individuals who are experiencing both success and failure.

Cyber-Flirting

After you start forming relationships online, you might find yourself flirting with others via your email, chat, and instant messaging communications. In addition to the playful conversation, double entendres, and possible sexual innuendo that are common in such encounters, the Internet has developed some tools for flirting online that are unique unto itself.

Emoticons

Emoticons, or smileys as they are often referred to, are little text-based pictures that can convey a feeling within your message (see Figure 4.4). Some common ones are:

Figure 4.3

Ryan Loos took his search for a girlfriend straight to the Internet by building his own Web page.

Emoticon	Description
:) or :-)	The original smiley that means "I'm happy." Can also mean "I'm joking."
:(or :-(	"I'm sad." Indicates to reader that the current writer is sad at what he or she has just heard.
;-)	A wink. Usually used for a flirtatious or sarcastic remark.
{} or []	A hug.
{{{***}}}	Hugs and kisses.

There is a heated debate over the use of smileys on the Internet. Some feel that they are ludicrous and completely slow down communication because you have to stop reading a message to figure out the meaning of each cryptic little cartoon. Others love the fact that they can clarify communications by conveying emotions, actions, and humor that might otherwise get lost in electronic communication. If you'd like to explore the hundreds (if not thousands) of smileys currently being used (or if you need to find the meaning of one), you can check out the following resources:

Online Lingo

http://www.thirdage.com/features/tech/netglos/index.html

Internet Smileys.... ^_^

http://members.aol.com/bearpage/smileys.htm

Smilies Unlimited

http://www.czweb.com/smilies.htm

Figure 4.4

Definitions for this emoticon, as well as others, can be found at the Online Lingo site located at `http://www.thirdage.com/features/tech/netglos/index.html`.

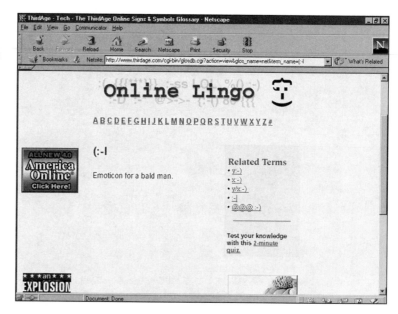

Whether you like emoticons or not, you might want to surf over to humorist Dave Barry's very funny article on using Internet "shorthand" at `http://www.randomhouse.com/features/davebarry/emoticon.html`. See if you can determine which of the emoticons he cites are actually being used and which are from his fertile imagination.

Acronyms

In addition to emoticons, Internet socializing is known for its acronyms. Commonly used in online chatting, these acronyms have made their way into emails, newsgroups, and instant messages as well. Some common acronyms are:

Acronym	Meaning
AFAIK	As far as I know
A/S/L	Age/Sex/Location (usually asking for yours)
BBL	Be back later
BTW	By the way
DIKY	Do I know you?
GAL	Get a life
GMTA	Great minds think alike
ILY	I love you
F2F	Face to Face
IRL	In real life
LOL	Laugh out loud

As with emoticons, your use of acronyms is purely a subjective decision. Here are some resources to learn and decipher the hundreds of additional ones:

Alphabet Soup Explained

http://members.aol.com/nigthomas/alphabet.html

Usenet Acronyms Dictionary

http://homepages.ihug.co.nz/~tajwileb/dictionary.html

V.E.R.A. (Virtual Entity of Relevant Acronyms)

http://userpage.fu-berlin.de/~oheiabbd/vera-e.html

(This is a search engine for acronyms.)

Signatures

As I mentioned in Chapter 3, "Was George Orwell Paranoid or an Optimist?" signatures are textual addendum to emails and other written online communications that can contain your name and other personal information. But many people use a signature to reveal an aspect of their personality or just to flirt. A signature can contain a quotation, saying, question, or statement that you find provocative or reflects who you are as a person. Almost every email program and most of the newsgroup and instant messaging programs these days allow signatures, so it can be a great flirtation tool when corresponding online. Just look up the word "signature" in your program's help area to see how to set one up. But remember, if you do set up a signature, whatever text you put in it will be sent out with every email, instant message, or newsgroup posting you generate.

Some people enjoy using signatures so much that they include pictures composed of typewritten characters within them. Much more complex than emoticons, these pictures, often referred to as ASCII art, can take hours to prepare (see Figure 4.5). Some sources for viewing and learning about ASCII art are:

Christopher Johnson's ASCII Art Collection

http://www.chris.com/ascii_art_menu.html

(This site has a tremendous collection of ASCII artwork plus tutorials on how to create your own.)

ASCII Art

http://www.home.aone.net.au/trezona/ascii.htm

The Great ASCII Art Library

http://www.geocities.com/SouthBeach/Marina/4942/ascii.htm

Figure 4.5

*Here are some examples
of ASCII art courtesy of*
`http://www.home.aone.
net.au/trezona/ascii.
htm.`

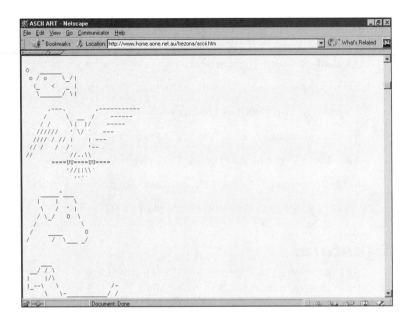

In case you were wondering, ASCII (American Standard Code for Information
Interchange) is the code many computers use for representing the printable characters on the keyboard as well as other information.

Venturing Forth

*Who are these people online? What's it like communicating with them? Do people
who meet each other over the Internet ever get together in person? And if they do,
what happens between them?*

*In an attempt to explore these and other questions about the actual process of
online dating and relating,* The Complete Idiot's Guide *will, throughout this book,
feature anecdotes from people who have already socialized via the Internet.
Entitled "From the Frontlines," these recollections will hopefully give you a sense of
what goes on when people meet online and sometimes take those relationships into
the offline world. Although each anecdote is signed, many of the names have been
changed to allow anonymity for the authors who have requested it. Our first "From
the Frontlines" is from a woman named Karen.*

continues

continued

"I considered myself pretty typical. An interesting, professional woman in her 30s living in New York who, for some unknowable reason, lacked a life partner. I had relied, without success, on meeting people the old-fashioned ways. I'd never placed or answered a personal ad. I'd never used a dating service. I'd never entered an online chat room. Such brazen solicitation was anathema to me. You can't mechanize love like it was a job search, I believed. I would rely on the fates, even though they seemed to be ignoring me.

But then my girlfriends started raving about their online dating experiences. One friend had a series of short-term relationships that began online, and had recently moved in with a man she met through a matchmaker Web site. Hell, they'd even bought a parrot together. What could be more of a commitment than a pet that lives 40 years?

So I thought I'd try it. To preserve my dignity, and lest I should appear desperate, I resolved to tell no one. This raised a hypothetical problem: What if I actually met my life partner online? How would I answer that first question—"So how did you meet?" Putting all that in the cross-that-bridge-should-I-be-so-lucky category, I started out with little hope of success. I told myself I would just see what it was like, see if anyone wrote to me. I gave myself permission to not respond to even a single email.

Setting aside a Saturday afternoon, I logged onto the site my girlfriend recommended. I was further emboldened to discover they offered a one-week free trial membership. Signing up, I resolved *not* to extend my membership after the week expired. I wasn't going to be so desperate as to pay for this, after all.

Writing in a hurry (some things shouldn't be labored over, I thought), I wrote my all-important profile, aiming to set the bar as high as I could. The upshot of my little paragraph was "I am magnificent and complicated. Don't apply if you're not up to me." I was seeking someone to be my match intellectually, emotionally, spiritually, and sexually. One-stop shopping. Going "live," I felt like an Amazon. They would come flocking to me.

Well, perhaps "flock" is not the right word. But come they did in all their infinite variety. Some married, some boasting of their yachts, some concerned about my body fat percentage, some intellectually challenged, and some just plain creepy.

Now that I had access to this vast personal ads database, I began perusing the men's profiles. Let me tell you, this is one of those glaze-over-and-quick activities. After reading about a dozen profiles, brevity became my Holy Grail. Forget mature, forget artistic, and forget generous and playful. The ability to get to the

continues

continued

point was now paramount in my search for a mate. I found myself skimming for key words (Theater, Zen, James Joyce equals "Hmmm. Let's go back and read that more closely." Walks on the beach, "looking for a lady" or "soul mate" equals "Next!"). I began sneering at the screen. The smallest misspelling was enough to make me hit Page Down. It seemed like 75 percent of the entrants could be dismissed on flawed spelling and grammar alone, without even considering the content of the profile. Is this what's out there? Smarmy married men who don't know the difference between "there" and "their?" Is this what I have to settle for? One otherwise promising painter tied his own noose by not even summoning the energy to hit the Shift key and start his sentences with a capital letter. Such a sluggard is never going to bring me chicken soup when I'm sick.

Nevertheless, I found three interesting men that I was compelled to write to (thereby chucking my promise not to send any emails just about an hour after making it). In the "Re" line of each of the three messages, I wrote, "How does it feel to be my first?" Clearly, I didn't fully consider the ramifications of beginning a relationship with a lie. I was having too much fun.

Two days into my free one-week trial, jockeying around with two or three fledgling correspondences, I got a message from a man. His was the first to tease me, to challenge the logic of my profile, and to engage intellectually. It was an enticing message.

Before writing back, I looked up his profile and found a *noir*-style meditation full of cleverly clunky metaphors on trying, but being unable, to write a profile. Now this was clearly the most winning posting I'd seen. Here was a man who was funny, creative, challenging, and could write like a dream. I neglected to think about the implications of someone who had posted a profile that told me nothing about himself. No facts, no likes and dislikes, and no physical attributes. Despite this—or perhaps because of it—I was intrigued. I wrote right back.

For three days, he and I engaged in a fun and highly satisfying correspondence. Each day, I eagerly opened my mailbox to see if he had written back, and each day he had, at length. He was funny and provocative. He had depth and self-knowledge. He was well read without being a show off about it. He told a good story. He wrote that he found my letters "enchanting." Call me easy, but I was utterly charmed.

On the fourth day of our correspondence, he suggested we talk on the phone. For an instant, I panicked. Offline after only three days? When things were going so well? Why spoil it? What if he's the proverbial ax murderer? What if he's

continues

continued

hideous to look at? What if he thinks I'm hideous to look at? What if everything he'd written was an intricate scaffold of lies?

Best to find out, then, isn't it?

At the appointed hour, queasy with nerves, I dialed the phone. When he answered, I heard a voice that was not what I expected. Someone so smart, so clever, so literary. In my infinite prejudice, I didn't imagine he'd have an accent. But he did. His verbal mannerisms threw me. While his emails seemed teasing and urbane, his conversation seemed pointed and quarrelsome. Describing himself, he said he was "an acquired taste." Talk about a red flag. Why didn't he just say, "don't expect to like me, but if you have endurance and can grit your teeth, you might find I'm palatable?" I was having some serious doubts.

Mike asked me if I thought we should meet. Despite my reservations, he *was* still the guy who wrote me those great emails. I considered his question. I paused for far too long, deer-in-the-headlights style. I felt sure I wouldn't like him. Not in the big way. Maybe email is its own arena. Maybe relationships there should stay there. Maybe the chemistry we spark with words is different from the chemistry that sends us spiraling when we're face to face. Maybe.

I said yes. Sure. Let's meet.

Two days later, Mike and I met for coffee and, despite my reservations, I was almost instantly taken. No aggregate of emails could capture the quirks, the gestures, the delivery, the irony, the sweetness, the smarts, the boyishness, in short, the highly unusual charm of this man. Yes, he did appear to be an acquired taste. But somehow I seemed to have already acquired it.

Call me lucky. By all reports, my experience was the exception. Most email relationships fall flat upon first, shall we call it *physical*, meeting. But Mike and I liked each other that first date, enough to go out again. And again. And so we dated for nearly three months.

In the end, though, we weren't precisely right for each other. Not in the big way. Perhaps there wasn't enough face-to-face chemistry. Perhaps there is a fundamental flaw in beginning a relationship online and trying to make things work offline. Or perhaps it was just like any other relationship. It might have worked, but it didn't.

—*Karen*

The Least You Need to Know

➤ When creating an online personal ad, write it before you go online. Try to concentrate on revealing your personality as well as facts about who you are.

➤ Some things to avoid when writing your online personal ad include making the ad a listing of clichés, negativity, and all the activities you enjoy.

➤ Make sure if you plan to exchange photographs with someone online or use a picture with your personal ad that the photo looks like you and is of good quality.

➤ The Internet has developed several ways to flirt that are unique to the medium. These include emoticons, acronyms, and signatures.

Chapter 5

Do You Type Here Often?

In This Chapter

➤ Personal ads sites that charge a fee

➤ Personal ads sites that are free

➤ Dating resources that can be found online

You've written your personal ad, you know what type of relationship you're looking for, and because you know how to socialize online in safety, you've got your fear under control. All that leaves is where to go to meet people. Most of the Web sites in this chapter are primarily personal ad sites that allow people to meet each other anonymously. They all cut a wide swath in regards to age, geography, sexual preference, and types of relationships offered.

Personal Ads Sites That Charge a Fee

Why, you might ask, would anyone pay to post a personal ad when there are so many sites that offer the same service for free? There are two good reasons. First, when sites are free, many of the ads placed are by people who are just experimenting with online dating or promoting agendas other than meeting people. This does not mean that there aren't people at the free sites who truly want to meet you (there are), but it does mean that you'll have a lot more dead weight to contend with in the guise of people not responding to your queries or looking to play games. Although most of the pay sites only charge a small monthly fee, this is usually enough to dissuade the people who are not truly interested in meeting others from joining.

The second reason to use a pay site is just as simple: Pay sites usually offer more or better services. The free personal ad sites usually just supply the basics of posting your ad, simple search capabilities, and maybe one or two other amenities. The pay sites often have unique features like automatic notification to your home email when a person who meets your criteria joins the site.

Many people, not surprisingly, explore both the pay and free personal ad sites. You'll discover that each site, pay or free, has its unique personality and attracts a clientele that fits its philosophy. Following are some online personal ad sites that charge a fee, but provide a lot in return.

Match.com

`http://www.match.com`

Since 1995 (virtually a historical span in Internet time), Match.com has been providing a safe, anonymous way for people to meet each other (see Figure 5.1). The site allows members to browse ads randomly or use a variety of search tools to locate prospective others by geography and gender, as well as by attributes that include type of relationship sought (Match.com divides this into the categories email pen-pal, activity partner, short-term relationship, and long-term relationship), age, ethnicity, religion, body type, height, and to the extent one drinks or smokes. Match.com makes no judgements on member sexuality as heterosexual, lesbian, and homosexual ads are all in evidence (and can be searched for exclusively as well). According to the site, Match.com's membership (which, as of this writing, totals more than 1.8 million since the site's inception) breaks down as follows:

➤ 78% are between the ages of 25 and 54

➤ 82% have attended college and 21% have advance degrees

➤ 52% are employed in managerial/professional fields

➤ 52% earn more than $40,000 a year

➤ 79% have no children

➤ 58% are single and have never married while 30% are divorced

How Match.com Works

Match.com provides interested parties with a one-week free trial, during which all the site's features can be explored. Those who continue their membership past the free trial period are charged a monthly fee (as of this writing, it starts at $16.95 per month and costs less as you purchase multiple months in advance). No credit card information is taken unless you decide to extend your membership during or after your free trial period.

Figure 5.1

Match.com provides one of the most safe and professional sites for meeting people nationally in the U.S. as well as in other countries.

Each member creates a handle to replace his or her real name. When a member sees a personal for someone he or she would like to correspond with, the member just sends an email to the address for the ad's anonymous handle—for example, JaneDoe@match.com. Match.com's computer strips away the sender's original email address and replaces it with their own substitute Match.com email address. In this way, the correspondents cannot contact each other at their everyday email addresses (or phone or home address) unless the information is shared voluntarily.

WARNING

Are You Really Anonymous?

When sending emails via services like Match.com that strip away your real email address, you still have to be careful not to give your identity away via signature files. Signature files are text closures that are appended to the end of emails in many corporate and home environments and are created automatically with each email sent. If you are unsure whether or not your email generates such text, which often includes the specifics of name, business phone number, and business address, send an email to yourself from that account. If no text was generated, your email is not creating a signature. If, however, it automatically sends out personal info, you need to disable it or acquire a free Web-based email account as discussed in Chapter 3, "Was George Orwell Paranoid or an Optimist?"

Match.com Perks

To place an ad on Match.com, each Match.com member fills out a profile that contains his or her personal ad, an optional photo, and descriptive information (race, religion, body type, and so on) for the ad writer and the desired match. It is these profiles that allow Match.com to offer Venus, an automated search agent. Venus, a no-extra-charge amenity, will automatically send an email to a member whenever a person who meets the criteria he or she is looking for joins the site. The email will list the possible match's handle, headline, gender, age, and general location. If the member wants to explore further, he or she returns to the Match.com site and searches for the handle of the person Venus suggested (see Figure 5.2).

Figure 5.2

Match.com's search utility allows you to find another member, even if you can't remember that person's anonymous handle.

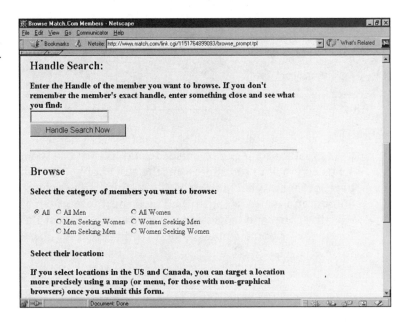

Match.com also lists within each member's profile the last date that person was active on the Web site. This is important so that you don't waste your effort writing to someone who hasn't been actively trying to meet someone for an extended time.

Match.com also facilitates member events, both in the physical and virtual worlds, as well as providing an e-zine (electronic magazine), "Mix'n Match," that chronicles online dating and the various offshoots of that activity. Lastly, it provides its own online chat forum for its members.

Matchmaker.com

`http://www.matchmaker.com`

It's not surprising that Matchmaker.com boasts more than 2.5 million members as of this writing (see Figure 5.3). The umbrella site for dozens of specialized personal ad sites, each devoted to a geographical location or special interest, Matchmaker has so many features and capabilities that you could spend days just learning how to use it. But unlike most of the sites in this chapter, which rely on the user to post a single personal ad containing the pertinent information he or she wants to relay, Matchmaker.com requires each user to answer 49 multiple-choice questions, ranging from the basics of your age range, gender, and sexual preference to sundry issues like your favorite type of music, whether or not you follow fashion, and your favorite season. As if that weren't enough, the site then offers 44 optional essay questions it strongly recommends you answer. These give you a chance to hold forth on your favorite toys as a child, what you find sexy, as well as a place for any additional comments the previous parts of the questionnaire didn't cover. What do you get for all this effort? In a word, plenty, but be prepared to invest some time and effort to get the most out of the site.

Figure 5.3

Matchmaker.com is a popular service that lets users meet people from around the globe and also caters to particular interest groups.

How Matchmaker.com Works

Before you fill out Matchmaker.com's questionnaire, you must first select which Matchmaker site you want to join. Most people choose one based on geographic location, but their network also contains the following special interest sites:

Religious Sites:

➤ Christian Connection

➤ Catholic Singles

➤ Latter Day Saints/Mormons

➤ Jewish Singles

Age-Related Sites:

➤ Teen-Talk

➤ College Connection

➤ Silver (over 40) Connection

Community Service Sites:

➤ Recovery Connection

➤ Long Term Care Connection

Lifestyle Sites:

➤ Swingers and Couples

➤ Gay/Lesbian Lifestyles

➤ Nudist Lifestyles

Like many dating sites, Matchmaker.com offers new members a free-trial period, which in this case varies from two to four weeks. During the free trial, members can use most of the site's functions, but are limited in the number of emails they can send to other members. They might also be barred from the site's chat rooms until they sign up for a paid full membership. Rates for MatchMaker.com, as of this writing, are $12.95/month when paying one month at a time, up to $99.95 for 12 months when paid in advance.

Matchmaker.com maintains anonymity and security without the use of an anonymous remailer by keeping all email to and from members on its Web site. This means that to do any Matchmaker activity, including corresponding with other members, you have to be logged onto the Matchmaker Web site with your browser. For some, this presents no problem; but for others who like the convenience of composing email offline, it can be irksome.

Many features make Matchmaker attractive to its members:

➤ A comprehensive search feature that utilizes the questionnaire, as well as other information

➤ A "Match" function that will list people whose questionnaire responses have matched yours

➤ An online diary to keep private notes on all the people you're communicating with

➤ Information telling you when the person was last active on the system and when his or her membership expires

➤ A very cool "Who's On?" function that tracks when members are on the system and allows you to chat with them (via the computer) immediately after reading their questionnaire answers

On the negative side, Matchmaker.com sometimes can be confusing to navigate. Also, it uses a three-letter designation, called the SPA, to identify a person's gender, sexual preference, and age range. This is handy for the seasoned Matchmaker user, but might make the newcomer yearn for clarity (for example, if your SPA is (AAD), the first A equals male, the second A equals heterosexual, and the third letter, D, equals an age range of 21-25). But these faults are minor for a service that provides a wealth of opportunities for those willing to put in the effort.

Cruising for Love

I started exploring the personal ads online as a means to meet other single sailors who shared my goal of cruising the world. As I was living aboard my own boat at the time, hoping to sell it in preparation for future voyages and unable to leave until then, I placed an "impossible" ad, one I believed no one would respond to. The ad I placed described my "ideal mate" with so many specific requirements and in such great detail (down to the person's height, hair, and eye color) that I didn't believe anyone could possibly fit the bill. And I was right. Almost. More than 500 people viewed my ad before I got one response! Then one day I received an email from a man who simply said "I am exactly what you are searching for except for my eye color. I could wear colored contact lenses."

I lived in San Francisco and he in Los Angeles, so we "dated" for a couple of months, chatting daily online with each other before I made my first weekend trip to Los Angeles to meet him in person. I sold my boat and we started to date seriously, but the travel between San Francisco and Los Angeles became rather tedious; so, 8 months after receiving his first email, I moved in with him to see if we could really live together. We were married 7 months later! We are now in the process of selling our house and readying our new boat for the next phase of our continued adventure together, which in all likelihood would never have occurred had it not been for the technology of the Internet!

—Carole

Mingles.com

http://www.mingles.com

Mingles.com has taken a middle-ground approach to its free trial policy. When you become a member, there is no fee for as long as you like. The catch: you can receive emails and respond to those you receive, but you cannot initiate contact directly from the site to any other members you find alluring. For the privilege of emailing people as you encounter their ads, you must purchase a "GOLD-level" membership, which costs, as of this writing, $7.99 per month and becomes cheaper with multiple months purchased in advance.

Mingles.com has many of the amenities of the previously mentioned sites (anonymous remailer, search functions, photo posting, email notification when other members who meet your criteria sign up, and so on), but it has one feature that's uncommon: voice messaging. Mingles.com allows members to post a voice recording with their personal ad by simply placing a phone call and recording your message live or by emailing them a recording of your voice digitized to a computer file. After your voice is posted to your ad, anyone with the proper software (RealPlayer G2 from RealNetworks, available for free download at http://www.real.com/products/player/index.html) can play it from the Web page it's posted on.

As if that was not enough, Mingles.com also features a chat environment called PhotoChat (see Figure 5.4) that displays a picture of each chat room participant next to each line of dialogue that is typed. For people who do not have a photo posted with their personal ad, PhotoChat supplies a selection of fun cartoon faces so members without photos are not left out.

Figure 5.4

Mingles.com's unique PhotoChat environment allows members to see who they are talking to, or at the very least, a cartoon recreation of that person.

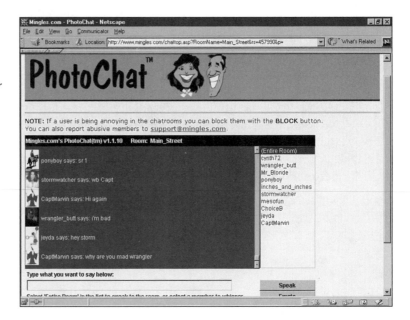

One & Only Internet Personals

http://www.one-and-only.com

One & Only is similar to the Mingles.com site, but with one exception: when you view a person's ad, there is no date stamp to tell you when the ad was posted or when the person was last active as a member. As such, when you write to someone, there's no way to tell if the ad has been on the system for three days, three months, or three years. And even though, like the other services, One & Only provides people with the ability to remove their ad, it's an unfortunate truth that people don't always clean up after themselves.

As far as pricing, One & Only lets you post an ad for free, but like Mingles.com, requires a paid membership to initiate contact with ads on their site. Paid member-ships, or AYCE (All You Can E-Mail), cost $24.94/month or less in increments of mul-tiple months purchased in advance. As always, these prices are subject to change.

metrodate.com

http://www.metrodate.com

Compared to the other online Web-based personals pay sites, metrodate.com is pricey. Placing your ad is free, but to contact others you have to purchase tokens, each one good for one correspondence to someone on their system. Token prices, as of this writing, start at $19.95 for a set of five and are discounted for advance pur-chases of greater numbers. In addition, when you contact someone, they are given your everyday email address.

metrodate.com also provides a matching service, much like matchmaker.com, where a lengthy questionnaire is filled out and you are matched with other like-minded souls, but unlike Matchmaker.com you are charged for each match starting at $14.95/match (also subject to change).

There were lots of things I didn't like about metrodate.com including the absence of a way to remove your ad once it's posted and a registration process that almost begs for a user to type the wrong password because there is no form of confirmation. These points, the high price and the comparatively small pool of available people to meet makes metrodate.com the one pay site in this list I recommend that you avoid.

Other Sites

Here are a few more personal ads sites that charge a fee that you might want to explore. They all feature some combination of the services discussed previously or ones that are similar.

A Love at First Site

http://www.aloveatfirstsite.com

Kiss.com

http://www.kiss.com

Love@1st Site

http://www.1st-site.com

webpersonals.com

http://www.webpersonals.com

Personal Ads Sites That Are Free

The beauty of trying to meet someone on a free Web-based personal ad site is just that: it costs nothing but your effort to try. For those who want to experiment with online personals, free sites offer a way to explore your comfort level with this dating environment without committing even a small amount of cash.

Yahoo! Personals

http://personals.yahoo.com

Yahoo! Personals was invented for those people who like their personal ad Web sites free of distractions (see Figure 5.5). A text-only site, members cannot post photos or voice messages next to their personal. But Yahoo! does allow you to list a Web page address (so people can find your picture on another Web site or just find out your surfing tastes) and provides complete anonymity by providing each user with the ability to create up to five Public Profiles. Each profile is an anonymous (if you choose) identity that can contain whatever information about yourself that you want to divulge. More importantly, when people respond to your ad, they email your identity, thus protecting your everyday email address.

Online socializers can get started with Yahoo! Personals by becoming a member of Yahoo! (as described in Chapter 3, under the section "Free Web-Based Email"). After you are signed up, you will see that any identity you create will have its own email box whose contents can be retrieved via the Web whenever you log onto Yahoo!

There is only one perk to Yahoo! Personals other than anonymity. If you use Yahoo! Messenger (see Chapter 11, "The Velvet Rope") to send and receive instant messages, Yahoo! will send you an instant notification whenever someone has replied to your personal ad.

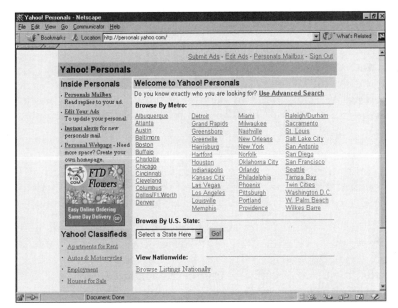

Figure 5.5

The welcome page for Yahoo! Personals has links to everything the service offers including personal ads from residents of all fifty U.S. states.

Oh So Young

Well, this might seem really twisted and warped, but I met a 28-year old guy online from the same city as me, and he seemed pretty nice, so I gave him my phone number. Sounds innocent? Not really. Well, you see, I told him that I was 19, but I was only 15. I dated him for like 4 months, with him thinking that I was 19. He invited me out to clubs and I'd say that I was sick so I couldn't go, but of course, I had no fake ID. He has even tried a few sexual things on me, but I refused him. He thought that I was just a nervous virgin. Well, from where I am from, you can't have sex until you're 16. So, I tried to abide by the law, although I knew what I was doing was very, very wrong.

He still doesn't know why I broke up with him.

—Ann

Excite Classifieds and Auctions

`http://www.classifieds2000.com`

As you might know, Yahoo! started as a search engine devoted to helping people locate Web sites of interest. As the Web has grown, Yahoo! and its competitors have developed into Web portals, Web sites that provide Web searching capabilities and a host of other services. As such, Excite, one of Yahoo's chief competitors, also supplies a similar free personal ad Web site.

When you arrive at the main page for Excite's classifieds, clicking the "Personals & Friends" link will take you to their personal ad search engine and a link for placing your own ad. They offer mostly the same services as the Yahoo! Personals, but with a slightly different user interface.

You might be tempted to check out the personal ads from other Web search engines or portals, but a surprise might await you. Many of the other services have forged agreements with established personal ads services to feature personal ads seen elsewhere on the Web. In the case of Lycos.com and Infospace.com, both services feature the One & Only Internet Personals discussed earlier, and Snap.com features Excite's classifieds.

Love@AOL Photo Personals

`http://www.love.com`

When America Online (AOL) started its personals in 1996, only those who used AOL's proprietary software and paid their monthly fee could access those ads. But AOL has been expanding its Web presence and making some content available to anyone with a Web browser. As such anyone with Internet connectivity can use AOL's Photo Personals, which gives you access to more than 250,000 personals culled from its membership of 20 million plus and the Internet community in general.

As the name suggests, users can supply a photo with their personal. When someone sees your ad, your everyday email address is listed under your picture (or the place-holder for the one that's not there). Interested parties can then contact you at your everyday email address or, if you followed the safety suggestion from Chapter 3, your anonymous Web-based email account. In addition, if both you and the person perusing your ad have AOL Instant Messenger (AOL's software for sending real-time messages covered in Chapter 11, "The Velvet Rope"), you can contact them via that function.

AOL's Photo Personals do not list when a person posted their ad or last used the Web site. If you are in your teens or twenties, AOL could be a good choice for you though, as there are a lot of ads from these age groups listed with the site.

Other Sites

Although there are literally dozens of other sites that offer free personal ads, many of them are just locally based, have few postings, or are not reliable. One good source for geographically desirable personals online is usually your local newspaper's Web site if it has one. These sites vary greatly in quality and services, but can offer a tremendous source for meeting people nearby, especially if you are located far from a metropolitan area. In addition to newspapers, I've listed two other national free personals Web sites you might want to explore. Please keep in mind that your selection of postings to browse, as well as the audience available to see your ad, might be limited or nonexistent depending on your location.

Swoon

http://www.swoon.com

relationships.com

http://www.relationships.com

Online Dating Resources

The problem with any book concerning the Web is that within the several months it takes to write, edit, publish, and get this book into your hands, dozens of new dating Web sites have appeared on the scene and dozens more have changed, merged with others, or ceased to publish. Fear not, for the following Web-based resources are dedicated to tracking the online dating scene and keeping you abreast of it.

About.com's Dating Advice Page

http://dating.about.com

About.com, an umbrella site for dozens if not hundreds of individual sites on specialized topics, is one of the great resources on the Web and its Dating Advice page is the cream of that crop (see Figure 5.6). Edited and compiled by Brenda Ross, this page has links and descriptions to some of the very best the Web has to offer for online daters. Updated every week, Ms. Ross describes and links to sites that have personal ads, love letters, dating advice (ranging from pick up lines to dealing with a break up), and much more. Rounding out its varied site listings and descriptions is an online chat forum and an advice forum bulletin board. If something of interest to people who date comes online, About.com's Dating Advice page is sure to have the skinny on it.

Figure 5.6

About.com's Dating Advice page at http://dating.about.com *is a constantly updated repository of the best that's going on in the online dating world.*

SingleSites.com

http://www.singlesites.com

Whereas About.com's Advice Page tries to bring the very best of online dating to its readership, SingleSites.com just tries to bring everything. Although it presents its listings of sites under various broad categories, finding a particular site could be frustrating. The listings aren't alphabetized, and there is no search engine. However, for the sheer scope of the good, bad, ugly, and alternative for online socializers, SingleSites.com makes fascinating browsing.

Cupid's Network

http://www.cupidnet.com

Similar to SingleSites.com, Cupid's Network also has a large selection of links to dating sites online.

Search Engines

Lastly, don't forget you can always check the various search engines like Yahoo! (http://www.yahoo.com) and goto.com (http://www.goto.com) to search for both new dating sites as well as new local and national personal ads sites.

The Least You Need to Know

➤ Personal ad Web sites that charge a fee usually provide more services than free sites and attract a clientele who is serious about meeting others.

➤ Free personal ad Web sites are a good starting place for people who want to experiment with online dating.

➤ Even though the Internet is ever-changing, there are a number of sites that keep track of the online dating scene providing surfers with up-to-date information on where and how to meet people online.

THAT GUY HAS JUST GOT **BAD NEWS** WRITTEN ALL OVER HIM.

Chapter 6

I Want Values for My Money

In This Chapter

➤ Personal ad sites based on religious preference

➤ Sites that cater to same sex personal ads

➤ Personal ad sites that cater to those with physical or mental challenges

➤ Special interest sites and how to be careful one is right for your personal ad

The more particular one is, the more useful the Internet will be for finding someone special. Although this chapter will start with some of the choices available to those looking to meet people who share a specific religious belief, it will also explore a host of Web sites devoted to meeting people based on special interest or sexual orientation.

Christian Sites

When looking at meeting people via Web sites based on a shared belief in Christianity, be sure the level of religious commitment of the site matches your own. Do you attend church once a month or are you evangelical? Should the person you're seeking just be Christian or have a more specific faith such as Roman Catholicism? These questions, of course, will more often than not determine your choice.

Christian Singles Connection

`http://www.cybergrace.com/html/singles.html`

One of the most telling facts about the Christian Singles Connection Web site (see Figure 6.1) is that 86% of its members attend church every Sunday. As of this writing, each of its more than 5,000 members pays no more than $6 per month (a full-year membership paid in advance is $36) to have access to the personal ads and pictures in its ever-growing database of Christian eligibles. Member profiles contain a personal ad as well as what denomination the ad-writer belongs to; whether his or her friends are mostly Christian, secular, or a mix of the two; and the member's favorite Bible personality, as well as other information.

Figure 6.1

The Christian Singles Connection boasts more than 5,000 members.

Christian Singles Commitments

`http://www.christiansingles.com`

Any site that opens its Web page with "Be ye not unequally yoked together with unbelievers," from II Corinthians 6:14 is fairly serious about its commitment to Christianity. Serving the Christian singles community since 1995, Christian Singles Commitments (CSC) (see Figure 6.2) has two basic requirements for membership:

1. You have accepted Jesus Christ in your heart as your personal savior.
2. You are a Christian marriage-minded single.

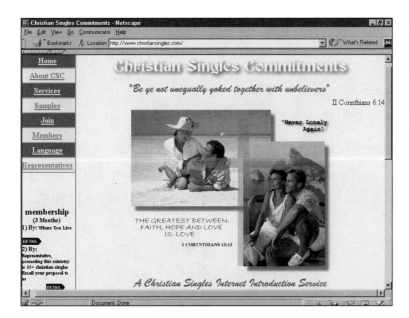

Figure 6.2

Christian Singles Commitments could be a good site to meet someone if you've accepted Jesus Christ as your personal savior.

Like many of the religious dating sites, CSC reserves the right to accept or reject any application, but after you become a member, monthly fees, as of this writing, vary from $5-$20 per month depending on the services you sign up for. They also offer various free three-month introductory memberships depending on the geographical location where you reside or your commitment to promoting the Web site to other groups of Christian singles. In addition to the placement of your personal ad, services include the posting of your photo, a matching service that pairs you with other marriage-minded Christian singles, a chat room, and the option to post a 30-second color video on the Web in which you relate basic information, as well as the story of how you were saved.

catholicsingles.com

http://www.catholicsingles.com

Having served more than 3,000 Catholic singles in its first year, catholicsingles.com provides all the basics of a personal ads site catering to a specific community. It provides its members with anonymous email, a chat room, and regularly updated links to news of interest to Catholics. The cost for members, as of this writing, is $8.95 per month, but it is free to all seniors 60 and over.

Other Sites

Here are a couple of other sites that might be of interest to the Christian dating community:

Christian Matchmakers International

`http://www.christianmatchmakers.com` (see Figure 6.3)

Figure 6.3

You can't take the dog out of dogma, or can you? This ad for Christian Matchmakers International tries.

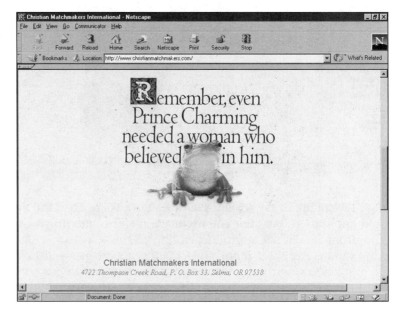

A Singles Christian Network

`http://www.singlec.com`

Jewish Sites

Ah, the plight of the Jewish mother who wants her son or daughter to marry within the faith. What is she to do? First, she must buy two copies of this book and give a pair to each of her children (one for home and one for the office). Then she is to direct them to this page where they will find a very nice selection of sites catering to Jews who want to meet other Jews. Tsores, she doesn't need.

Do You Know Enough About a Web Site?

All Web sites that provide a service—personal ads or otherwise—should have contact information clearly posted so that people with questions not answered online can seek further information. (At the very least, this information should include an email address, although many of the bigger sites have multiple ways to be contacted.) This way, should you have a question about a site's fee schedule, membership criteria, or services, you can send a query before committing your time or money. If a site is lacking contact information, that usually is indicative of a poorly run site. Never spend money or join a Web site unless all your questions have been thoroughly answered.

Jdate The Jewish Singles Network

`http://www.jdate.com`

Jdate could teach many of the other sites a thing or two about specificity. When a person places their ad with the site, they fill out the standard registration form listing basic information (see Figure 6.4). But where other sites provide only four or five choices for describing one's body type, Jdate provides 17 choices for women and 16 for men. Ten choices of hair color and 13 choices for eye color are provided. And not forgetting their mission of bringing Jewish singles together, each member lists religious background (11 choices), average synagogue attendance, and the degree to which one keeps kosher.

The cost for placing an ad with Jdate is free, but they charge you to contact others. As of this writing, fees range from $39 for three months of unlimited emailing to other members and use of all the site's features to a token system where each email you send costs one token which you purchase in groups of five or ten. Oddly enough, tokens can be purchased online, but memberships must be purchased by phone or postal mail.

Like many of the sites that cater to specific communities, Jdate does not list within the profiles of their members when they were last active on the service either browsing other ads or emailing members. Member profiles can list up to five photos and five personal essays. Jdate also provides a chat room and bulletin boards for its members.

Figure 6.4

Jdate's registration form can tell prospective surfers a lot about you.

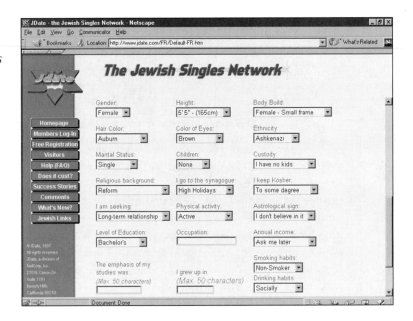

Jewish Quality Singles

http://www.jqs.com

Those who join Jewish Quality Singles' site are fairly serious about meeting someone. Membership fees (which are not displayed until the time of registration) start, as of this writing, at $125 for a six-month membership and there is no free-trial period. You can browse the profiles of members prior to joining, but no contact can be made until you've paid your fee and posted your personal. Many of the member profiles feature one or more photos (again, probably because the cost of membership dissuades dabblers) and the membership is from various countries. Each member is assigned a user ID number and all email communications are anonymous and must be retrieved from the Jewish Quality Singles Web site.

If there is one thing Jewish Quality Singles lacks, it is probably a more specific search engine. As of this writing, members can search based only on gender, age, country/continent, or by knowing a member's exact ID number. This means if you are looking for a female, age 30-39, who lives in Ohio, you must look through all the listings for women of this age group who live in the United States. Unlike other services, there are no facilities for narrowing down the search parameters. On the plus side, the site is very well designed and provides a focused service for a specific community.

The Jerusalem Post Personals

`http://www.jpostpersonals.com`

Although you might think the ads contained on its site are restricted to Israel's populace, The Jerusalem Post Personals boasts more than 15,000 members the world over
(see Figure 6.5). Moreover, it is not a strictly Jewish site, accepting ads from people of
all religions. But because there are a great many ads from Jewish people looking to
meet other Jews, it is a great online resource for that community.

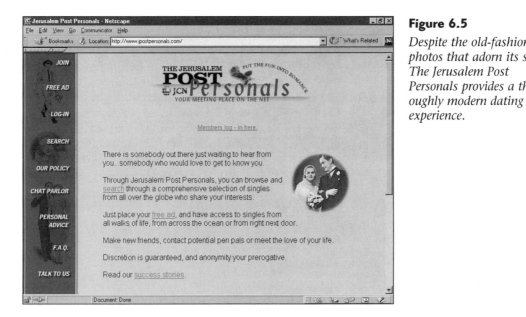

Figure 6.5

*Despite the old-fashioned
photos that adorn its site,
The Jerusalem Post
Personals provides a thoroughly modern dating
experience.*

Placing ads is free, but sending emails to other people and replying to emails you
receive from others requires that you become a paid member. Full membership starts,
as of this writing, at $9.95 per month and goes down in cost with additional months
purchased in advance.

The Jerusalem Post Personals provides complete anonymity with members retrieving
their mail directly from the site and it sends email notices to your everyday email
account when your ad has received a response. The site also takes a nice middle
ground to informing you whether a person whose ad you are browsing is still actively
seeking to meet someone online. Above the text portion of each profile is listed the
most recent week that the person logged on to the site (this week, last week, six weeks
ago, and so on). Like many of the other sites, The Jerusalem Post Personals provides a
chat room and some articles on dating advice. It should also be noted that The Jewish
Personals located at `http://www.jewishpersonals.com` is the same site under a different name.

Other Sites

Here are a couple of other sites that might be of interest to the Jewish dating community:

Ark Electronic Shadchenter

http://www.arkline.com

YiD (Your Ideal Date) Jewish Internet Dating

http://www.yid.com

More Personal Ads Sites Based on Religion

There are, of course, many religions other than Judaism and Christianity, although they are not as well represented by personal ad sites. Fortunately, many of the sites mentioned in Chapter 5, "Do You Type Here Often?" have subsections or features catering to particular religions. For example, Matchmaker.com has a special community for Latter-day Saints, and Match.com provides those who follow Buddhist, Hindu, or Islamic traditions with specific search criteria to enable members to locate like-minded souls within its community. This is not to say that other personal ad sites based on religious preference do not exist. Following are a few sites that cater to Muslims and Latter-day Saints. If you practice and would like to meet someone from these faiths, refer to the following sites.

Latter-day Saints Personal Ad Sites
LDSonline

http://www.ldsonline.com

It's rare to find an online personal ads site that caters to a singular community with a high level of proficiency at no charge, but that's exactly what LDSonline provides to Latter-day Saints looking to meet someone of the same faith. An international service, LDSonline features many amenities, including use of an anonymous remailer; the ability to search for matches on many criteria, including geographic region, relationship type sought, and religious affiliation; and the option for members to post their photo. Like some of the other personal ad sites, LDSonline performs all its searches by matching the member's profile against others who belong to the site. So, after you become a member of LDSonline, fill out your member profile. If you don't, most searches you perform will be alarmingly empty of prospective matches.

LDS Singles Online

http://www.ldssingles.com

LDS Singles Online claims they have posted more than 37,000 personal ads since the site's inception in 1996. This is not surprising considering the features offered by the site, including chat rooms, existing member notification when new members join the site, and offline events such as short cruises. What is surprising is that on occasion the site has technical difficulties with its free preview registration system and has, at times, trouble having its pages interpreted by Netscape Communicator. These caveats aside, LDS Singles Online charges, as of this writing, $8 for a one-month membership with the fee being reduced for multiple months purchased in advance.

Muslim Personal Ad Sites
Muslim Matrimonial Link

http://www.4you.com/MML

Whether you are Muslim, Sunni, or any other adherent of Islam, Muslim Matrimonial Link has those looking to meet you for a lifetime commitment. Like the best á la carte menus, the service charges only for what you use. As of this writing, two options for placing an ad exist: "Pay Per View" and "Pre Paid." In the Pay Per View plan, ads cost $5, but if a member wants to contact you after reading your personal, they must pay $1 to see your contact information. In the Pre Paid plan, ads cost $30, but other members view your contact information at no additional charge. Muslim Matrimonial Link also offers anonymous mailboxes, posting a photo with the ad, and the editing of existing ads all for additional fees (although they offer linking your ad to a photo elsewhere on the Web for free). An ad can be posted indefinitely as long as a member checks the status of it by going to the site at least once every two weeks. If this is not done, the ad is removed from the site.

Rishtay Free Internet Matrimonial for Muslims

http://www.metric.net/rishtay

Rishtay Free Internet Matrimonial for Muslims provides a basic text-only personals site for all single Muslims. Because the service is completely free, it is not surprising that extra features such as an anonymous remailer are not offered. It does, however, provide articles on marriage and links to other Islamic sites. There are two ways to locate ads on the international service: via a search utility and via links labeled "Brothers" and "Sisters" that allow one to peruse ads based on gender and time of month placed. However, I recommend going straight to the search engine because the Brothers/Sisters links can sometimes return little or no information.

Same Sex Personals

Lesbians and homosexuals looking to meet others who share their sexual orientation can meet that population via any of the sites listed in Chapter 5, "Do You Type Here Often?" But for those who would be more comfortable in an online setting devoted to same-sex communities, look no further than the following sites.

Gay Match Maker

http://www.gaymatchmaker.com

Gay Match Maker (see Figure 6.6) is one of the best examples of a Web service serving a community with specific needs. Each member who places an ad on the service (currently free, but mulling over the possibility of charging a small one-time registration fee) fills out a questionnaire that details everything from sexuality (gay, lesbian, bisexual, transgender, transsexual, drag queen, or won't say) to listing the most important component of a relationship and rating the importance of several dozen activities. After the questionnaire and your written personal are posted on the system, it matches you with others residing in the location you requested. All communication is handled by the system anonymously and you must retrieve messages from the Web site.

Figure 6.6

Gay Match Maker provides a top-notch online personal ad service.

One of the things that makes Gay Match Maker preferable to other personals Web sites is that it purges ads off its system if the user has not been active on the site for seven days. This means you are assured that any person you contact with Gay Match Maker has been actively searching to meet people within the last week.

Other amenities included in Gay Match Maker are an excellent online help section, a rating system that lets you know how closely your questionnaire answers pair up with prospective others, a chat room, an advice column, and message boards.

Edwina

http://www.edwina.com

Edwina is everything a personal ads site should be: Elegant yet easy to maneuver around in and with a personality that's well defined but doesn't stand in the way of its purpose (see Figure 6.7). Posting an ad is free, as is writing to others on the site, but if you want to read any email received as a result of your ad or queries to others, you'll need to pay $4.95 per month, although, as always, prices are subject to change.

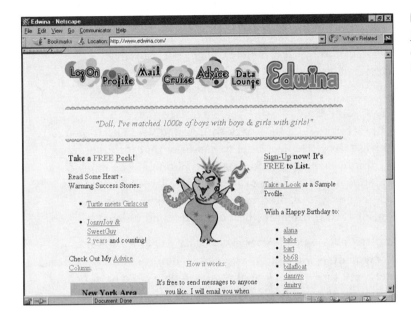

Figure 6.7

Edwina provides a fun, colorful interface to finding a same-sex partner.

Although Edwina doesn't sport many perks, it does offer an advice column and a direct link to The Data Lounge (http://www.datalounge.com), a premiere lesbian/gay news site that was created by the same company that operates Edwina. If there is one thing Edwina lacks, it is some sort of tracking device that tells users browsing ads when the writer of each personal was last active on the system.

Nu? Yenta

http://www.nuyenta.com

If you're Jewish and gay or lesbian, Nu? Yenta is the place to be. Another extremely well-implemented site, it provides anonymity, tracking when a user was last active on the system, and many more features. There's no charge to place an ad, but as of this writing it costs $9.95 per month to send and reply to email. Each profile not only lists the obligatory information, but also reveals a person's level of religious commitment, level of observance, and whether he or she keeps a kosher home.

Two Sides of the Same Coin

As a gay man, although only recently out, I found the anonymity of being online helped me explore a world I wasn't ready to fully enter. I had spent five months communicating online with someone from Seattle (I'm in Los Angeles). In the course of that time, we had amazing conversations and found we had a lot in common. The communication was first merely online, but soon included phone calls. After almost half a year, we decided to meet. I offered to go to Seattle and have dinner with him so we could celebrate our birthdays, which are on the same day.

It was a good, but not great evening. I flew back to L.A. and we talked again just prior to another trip I was taking. He asked me to call from that location, but after I did, I never heard from him again. No email, no phone call to explain his position, merely the disappearing act. Eight or nine months later I got an instant message from him while online. He wanted to explore a friendship with me, nothing more. That was fine. Unfortunately, he quickly became unreliable again.

Luckily, I have met another man online. After exchanging emails for a week, we met. He was immediately smitten with me. We agreed to have dinner again. Although I took a little more time to be sure about my feelings, we have been going strong for five months. Although we have had our share of rough moments (what relationship hasn't?), I'm feeling very good about the future of this relationship.

—Derek

Special Challenges

People who are mentally and physically challenged by disability, disease, or chronic illness are finding the Web an exciting place to try to meet people who have or understand the challenges they face. Here are a few sites notable for addressing the needs of these communities.

D.A.W.N. (Differently Abled Winners Network)

`http://www.azstarnet.com/~dawnser/netrel.htm`

Although not a personal ads site per se, I've included it here because D.A.W.N. essentially provides that service to those who are physically and mentally challenged.

Challenged adults, as well as nonchallenged adults wanting to meet members of the challenged community, can request an application for the service online. After the form has been filled out and mailed to D.A.W.N. with an initial payment (fees start at $79.95 for three months as of this writing), an interview is arranged and the organization goes about finding your match. More akin to traditional matchmaking than an online personal ads site, D.A.W.N. is reaching out via the Web to help this unique community.

Worldfriends

http://www.ampulove.com/worldfriends.htm

Unlike D.A.W.N., Worldfriends goes the traditional personal ads route for the physically challenged community. The site is mostly populated with ads from amputees and those who want to meet them, no doubt the result of being run by Ampulove, a Belgium organization devoted to helping that community. Although the site is in English, certain maneuvering aspects have been lost, no doubt due to translation (for instance, the announcement "Place your free adjunct now" adorned by the link "Place your advertise" directs you to the form to post your personal). Ads are free, but there is no date information as to when the ad was posted or when the writer was last actively looking to meet people.

Deaf World Web Talks

http://dww.deafworldweb.org/chat/index.html

The Deaf World Web, a central Internet clearinghouse for information concerning the deaf and hard-of-hearing communities, has started a personal ads section on a trial basis. When you encounter the site's opening page, it will appear devoted to discussion forums, but scrolling down will reveal a form for searching the ads and a link to place your own. Ads are free and users must publish an everyday email address to be contacted. Each ad lists the date it was posted and when it will expire (ads expire from one to eight weeks after placement, depending on the writer's wishes) as well as the writer's hearing identity (deaf, hard of hearing, sign-language student, and so on). Unfortunately, as of this writing, the site risks offending visitors as it uses the word "queers" to refer to those seeking homosexual or lesbian relationships. Hopefully, the site will revise its terminology, as otherwise it provides a useful service.

Living Positive HIV Dating Online

http://www.livingpositive.com

Straightforward is probably the best word to describe the Living Positive site, which provides free personals for the HIV Positive community. With no questionnaires or registration forms to fill out, just go to the link labeled "Post Page" and write what you want in a simple text box. Be sure to include an everyday email address, as there are no anonymous remailing facilities included in the site. You can even include a picture with your ad by submitting an attachment via email.

MPwH (Meeting People with Herpes)

http://www.antopia.com/herpes/MPwH

If you have genital herpes, MPwH is the first site to check out to meet others who are similarly challenged. Ensuring complete anonymity, the site assigns an identification number to each ad. When someone wants to contact an ad writer, he or she addresses an email to the ID number via the site. Emails are redirected to your everyday email account. If you want to respond, you then must reveal your public email address to the sender.

Listing an ad is free, as is receiving responses to a personal you've posted. If you want to contact ads directly, there is, as of this writing, a monthly charge of $7. MPwH also offers a hardship program, which grants a free three-month membership for those who cannot afford the monthly fee. Amenities include a chat room, a herpes dating community featuring message boards (hosted by Excite.com), and listings of social groups to meet people with herpes around the country.

Selective Beginnings

http://www.haveherpes.com

People living with genital herpes who want to meet other people with herpes can also turn to Selective Beginnings. As of this writing, women may post their ads for free and men pay $10 per month with a minimum three-month commitment. All ads come with anonymous email accessed directly from the site via Web browser. The site also offers a 1-900 telephone number that people can use to respond to ads, although at $1.99 per minute (average call around four minutes), this can add up. There is no "last date of activity" tracking, so there is no way to tell how long the free ads from women have been on the system.

Special Interest Sites

In the last few years, in an attempt to carve out a niche in the online personal ads market, dozens of sites appealing to people with particular interests or predilections have been launched (see Figure 6.8). Although these sites might be appealing because of the community they attract, it is best to approach them with a cautious attitude.

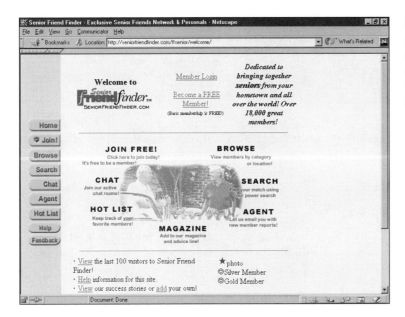

Figure 6.8

Senior FriendFinder is only one of many sites catering to a community with a shared special interest.

Many special interest sites have what are called live-forever ads—personals that the writer lost interest in long ago, but have not been removed. I found one of these on AfricanMatch (described next). A young lady had written a personal that also referenced her own Web site. When I visited her home page, I discovered she had already been married for two months and was no longer interested in finding the mate she advertised for. Other sites lack membership, and as such, provide a very small pool of people to meet. And finally, some are difficult to maneuver through or technically deficient in some way.

The following sites, and others that cater to a special community, might very well offer what you are looking for. But before committing money, time, or Web space to a special-interest personal ads site, be sure you find out the following information:

➤ How much does it cost? Are there any hidden fees?

➤ How do I remove my ad if I no longer want it? Is there an automatic function for this, or do I have to send correspondence requesting removal?

➤ Can I edit my ad after I've submitted it?

➤ Does the site provide anonymity?

➤ Is my private information kept private? Does my information get released to other companies?

➤ Is there a place to go for help online if I am having trouble with the site? Is there a place or person to contact if I am having trouble with the site or the charges placed to my credit card?

➤ Does the community of potential contacts provided by the site justify any expense I incur monetarily or via time and effort?

Some of the following sites do not answer the previous questions to my satisfaction. Only you can decide whether they are right for you.

AfricanMatch

http://www.africanmatch.com

A personal ads site devoted to bringing together Africans, African descendents, and non-Africans who "appreciate the culture, tradition, and moral values that are unique to Africa."

AstroMate

http://www.astromate.com

AstroMate matches you with others based on your astrological profile, as well as allowing you to browse or search through their member profiles.

Starmatch International

http://www.starmatch.com

Another personals site that measures compatibility via the astrological profiles of those involved.

Concerned Singles

http://www.concernedsingles.com

Concerned Singles brings together "progressive, socially conscious men and women who care about social justice, the environment, gender equity, racism, and personal growth."

IbnButata.com

http://www.ibnbatuta.com

The online singles site that features personals from Arabs, people of Arab descent, and their friends.

Large Encounters

http://www.large-encounters.com

If you are a plus-size lady or an admirer of big women, this site will take your personal ad.

Large and Lovely Connections

`http://www.largeandlovely.com`

Unlike Large Encounters, Large and Lovely connections is for both BBWs (Big Beautiful Women) and BHMs (Big Handsome Men), as well as their admirers.

Salt and Pepper Singles

`http://www.saltandpeppersingles.com`

Looking for an interracial relationship? Salt and Pepper Singles posts personal ads from those seeking one.

Senior FriendFinder

`http://seniorfriendfinder.com`

Although seniors have many resources to meet others, this site caters exclusively to that community.

Sex Classifieds & International Personals

Strewn throughout the Web are dozens of personal or quasi-personal ad sites for people wanting to meet women and men (although mostly women) who live overseas. Other Web sites list personal ads for people advertising for sex. Although both these types of personal ad sites might fulfill what you are looking for, I cannot recommend any. Many of these sites are populated with fake ads to lure unsuspecting rubes into paying a membership fee to join in the hopes of getting something they desperately seek for a relatively small amount. Other sites that belong to these categories, although they are legitimate, are abused by the site members, who place ads for their own pay-sex sites or offer prostitution. Especially heinous are the international personal ad sites that sell individual addresses of correspondents who are often paid to write back to American men in order to get them to spend more money on translation services, package tours to meet foreign cuties, and other services that are conveniently provided. To make matters worse, some sites mix legitimate overseas personals with fake ads to make the selection seem greater. Unfortunately, there are so many variations on the types of scams employed by these international personal ads sites that they would fill a separate book. And, although there are legitimate international and sex personal ad sites, the reliability of these sites can change rapidly, often due to companies changing ownership.

For those who desire to meet someone overseas, many of the sites in Chapter 5, "Do You Type Here Often?" as well as in this chapter, have large international memberships. As for those looking for sex or the fulfillment of sexual fantasies, these same sites will often host ads for all manner of sexual liaison.

If you do decide to explore the international personal ad sites or sex classified ads not discussed in this book, do so with extreme caution. They are easily found by using your favorite search engine to search for "sex personals" or "international personals." After you start exploring the sites, be sure you ask yourself the questions outlined in the section of this chapter entitled "Special Interest Sites." Also determine whether the site charges a fee to those listing their ads. Are both genders represented? Are there hidden fees? And last, is the company that runs a site located in the United States and is it accountable to U.S. law (although you shouldn't place much faith in this because proving legal infractions by these sites has been extremely difficult)?

The Least You Need to Know

➤ There are dozens of sites that cater to people who want to meet others based on religion, sexual preference, and other interests.

➤ The Internet provides a means for those with physical or mental challenges to meet others like themselves.

➤ Not all sites are created equal and you should know before placing your personal ad on a site whether it charges fees, ensures anonymity, has procedures for removing your ad when you are finished, and many other pieces of information.

Chapter 7

How Do I Love Thee? Let Me Modem the Ways

In This Chapter

➤ Online resources for revealing your feelings anonymously

➤ Courting online with poetry and kisses

➤ Courting online with humor

➤ Virtual postcards to send to loved ones

Courting the New-Fashioned Way

So, you've met someone you like. How do you show this person how you feel? Sure, there are the old standbys—candy, flowers, adjustable wrenches—but what if you've only met this person online? How can you move the relationship along without actually being in offline contact? Well, the World Wide Web has become a primary tool for romancing others whether you know them online or off.

Test the Waters

Perhaps there's someone you think is kinda cool. Kinda neat. Kinda someone who should be with you. But this person doesn't know you exist. Or you're friends and you think revealing your feelings could ruin an otherwise wonderful, albeit frustrating, relationship. Two Web sites, eCRUSH (see Figure 7.1) and SecretAdmirer.com, have come up with somewhat similar solutions to your romantic problem.

Figure 7.1

Can't stand the thought of rejection? Perhaps eCRUSH can help.

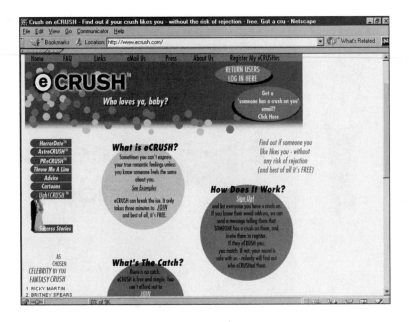

eCRUSH

`http://www.ecrush.com`

eCRUSH's premise is simple. When you register with the site, you record the name or names (if you're busily having multiple crushes) of those you have your eye on. You also optionally enter their email addresses and geographic location. If you entered the email address of your crush, that person is invited to the site with an automatically generated message from eCRUSH that alerts him or her to your interest without revealing your identity. If your intended registers and puts your name down as his or her desired honey, you will both get an email inviting you back to the site so that eCRUSH can reveal you as each other's crush. Even if you don't know the object of your affection's email address, both your names stay in eCRUSH's database, and should your future loved one independently register, a match can be recorded that way as well.

SecretAdmirer.com

`http://www.secretadmirer.com`

Unlike eCRUSH, SecretAdmirer.com needs the object of your affection's email address to make a match. After you've sent your intended a form letter from the site that informs him or her of an anonymous admirer, the recipient must then guess who his or her secret admirer is and then send that person a message from SecretAdmirer.com. After people have sent an anonymous email to each other, SecretAdmirer.com reveals the match. If, by chance, the recipient sent an anonymous email to a different person than the original Secret Admirer, the cycle starts all over again.

Convey Your Feelings

After you've found someone to romance online, it's sometimes hard to find the right words or gestures to make your feelings known. The following Web sites can assist you.

Cyrano Server

`http://www.nando.net/toys/cyrano.html`

If you liked Mad Libs, you'll feel fondly toward Cyrano Server, an automated Web-based letter writer (see Figure 7.2). After choosing the type of letter desired (Valentine, love letter, or breakup note), you fill out a form listing parts of speech and objects as well as proper names for you and your intended. Cyrano composes the letter, which you can choose to send or cancel. Prior to sending the letter, you can adorn it with graphics, sounds, and animations. After you send it, the recipient gets an email directing them to pick up his or her letter at the Cyrano Server Web site.

Figure 7.2

Let Cyrano write your way into someone's heart.

Passions in Poetry

`http://netpoets.com`

Under the right circumstances, nothing says "I'm thinking about you" better than the appropriate poem. Passions in Poetry has given poets currently producing work a place to deposit their writings for the world to read. Divided into categories such as "Sad Poems" and "Poems About Life," each original work has a link below it to send the poem to a friend. Of course, any poem you send can be accompanied by a note from you. The site also features hundreds of the most famous classic poems from heavy hitters such as Shakespeare and Wordsworth; surprisingly, however, these do not have automatic links to send them to a friend, forcing those who want to send those poems to do so manually by copying them into manually composed emails. Site tip: If you're looking for the funkier poems, click the link for the "Poetry Buffet."

E-Kisses

`http://www.thekiss.com/ekiss`

The fine folks at TheKiss.com have come up with two nifty ideas for courting online. The first, sending an E-Kiss (see Figure 7.3), enables you to compose a message and put in a graphic word balloon coming from a pair of lips that stands in for your personality. As in Cyrano Server, the recipient gets an email telling him or her to go to a Web page to retrieve your message.

Figure 7.3

E-kisses, such as this one, let your lips do the talking.

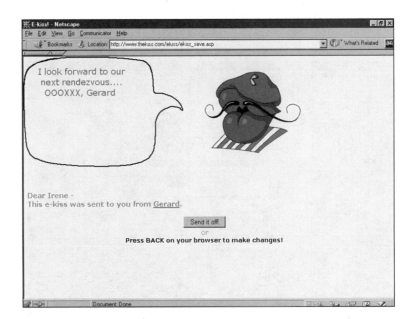

Kiss-Coupons

`http://www.thekiss.com/trunk/downloadables.asp`

You can also send someone a Kiss-Coupon. The coupons are actually designed to be printed out and given in person, but because they are graphic images, you can download them and send them as email attachments. To download a coupon with Netscape Communicator or Internet Explorer, just go to the image of the coupon and right click with your mouse. In Netscape choose the Save Image As command or in Explorer the Save Picture As command. After you email your Kiss-Coupon, all that remains is for you to supply the final product when your amour redeems it.

Kissogram

`http://www.kissogram.com.au`

If sending a pair of fancy lips is not enough, the Kissogram offers to send the object of your affections a moving image of a person giving him or her a kiss. Although I was instantly in love with Geekgirl, there is a wide selection of proxies ranging from temptresses to punk rockers, all of whom have offered their moving image of a kiss to the screen (see Figure 7.4). As with the other romantic offerings, the recipient retrieves his or her Kissogram (accompanied by a note from you) from the Web site.

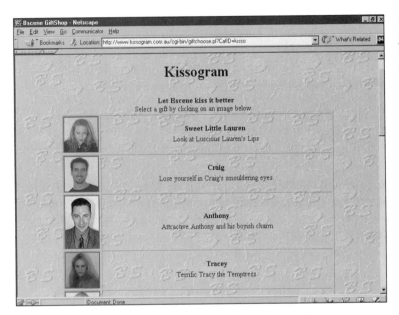

Figure 7.4

Just a few of the surrogates who will send a Kissogram to the one you want.

The Cyber-Subway

"Christmas Eve: I was on date number three with a guy I had initially met online who was boring me to tears. Nice guy, stiff as a starched suit, conversation sparkless. We had just come from dinner in Chinatown and a Klezmer concert. Though it was a frigid night, I suggested we walk the 15 or so blocks back to my car/his apartment, but he preferred to take the subway two stops. I succumbed. Reluctantly. At the first stop, a man and a woman entered our virtually empty car and sat diagonally across from us. I eyed the man doing a little happy jig with his feet on the floor beneath him. The two of them were smiley and animated, which stood in stark contrast to the flatness in our camp. The man looked vaguely familiar, too, and as the train approached our stop and we walked past them to the door, I apologized to him for staring but said that he looked familiar. He said I did, too. We introduced ourselves and realized simultaneously that we had gone out on a blind date about a year before.

He gave me a warm smile and handshake as my date and I slipped through the closing subway doors.

Outside in the street, I told my date that the other guy and I had had a terrific blind date, but that he had cancelled our second date because a relationship had unexpectedly taken off with some other woman in the interim. I proceeded to babble to my date about how much easier first dates are than second and especially third dates. How on first dates it's usually pretty easy to go through all the initial family and job crap, but that date three is more of a test of a meaningful connection. I was trying to hint about our lack of one.

Needless to say, I never saw him again. But Mr. High Energy Subway Man did call me the next day. He was with his sister on the subway the night before, he told me. He is no longer dating the woman he dumped me for a year ago. And do I want to go out. Thank you, fateful subway ride! We made a date for the following Tuesday evening. Tuesday morning, I got an email through the same dating Web site where I had met starched-suit-boring guy. It was from Subway Man! Though he had no idea it was me, I recognized him from his unusual name, with which he had signed his email. That evening, we had yet another terrific date, during which we laughed about what a small world it is and how we kept running into each other online and off.

On the next date the following week, he warned me that he is getting over a recent ex (yet another), and is not emotionally available. Caught up in the giddy newness of using these Internet dating services, though, he turned me on to another Web site devoted to online personal ads. Though less giddy and more jaded than he, I logged on. And logged off with him."

—Claudia

Make Your Intended Laugh

Although the Web is teeming with humorous sites, here are a couple you can use to assist you in the ways of courtship.

Funny.com

`http://www.funny.com`

There's nothing like a good laugh to help grease the wheels of a relationship and Funny.com tries to provide just that. A Web repository of jokes submitted by its members, Funny.com allows anyone who signs up for a free membership to email any joke from the site to whomever you want. Jokes are divided into categories (politics, relationship, religion, and so on) and ratings (as in movies: G, PG, R, and X) to assist finding the one that suits your needs.

Quote-O-Matic

`http://www.slip.net/~jmmallon/quotes/quote.html`

I wish I had one share of Microsoft stock for every time someone told me as a child, "If you can't say something nice, say nothing at all." Although this wisdom has served me well in the offline world, it has made some of my email correspondences rather pithy. To the rescue comes the Quote-O-Matic. Issuing forth a notable droplet of humor or common sense taken from mostly offline sources, the Quote-O-Matic can provide you with some very clever repartee to include in your online communications.

Send an Electronic Postcard

One of the original ways to flirt on the Web, the electronic postcard (or greeting card), is still extremely popular. So popular, in fact, that there are hundreds, if not thousands, of sites that enable you to send a pictorial greeting via the Internet. The six discussed here all basically work the same way: Pick the graphic or image that accompanies your card and compose a message and, when finished, the recipient receives an email directing him or her to a Web site to view the finished card. It should also be mentioned, all the following sites offer this service for free.

Mail A Meal

`http://www.mailameal.com/`

Mail A Meal (see Figure 7.5) is exactly what it sounds like—hundreds of postcards devoted to sending your intended the very best in food and beverage.

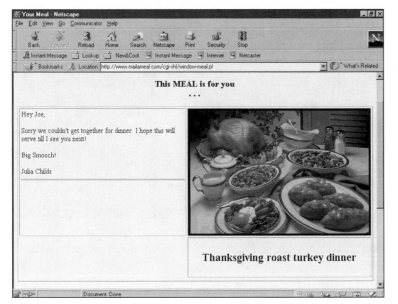

Figure 7.5

There's nothing tastier than letting Mail A Meal email your loved one a fine meal.

Shawna's Virtual Flowers

`http://drew.netusa1.net/~shawna/virtual`

Real flowers wither and die, but virtual flowers are a joy forever. Or until the Web page they are on expires. In any case, Shawna's Virtual Flowers has a huge selection of arrangements for every occasion to send with your card. And as an added bonus, you can also arrange for the card's Web page to provide a link to play a musical selection of your choice.

Virtual Vacation

`http://www.virtual-vacation.com`

Perhaps the person you want to court has the travel bug? Then Virtual Vacation, with its hundreds of photos of vistas from around the globe, can send an image that will surely bring joy to the recipient. The site will even notify you when the recipient has picked up his or her card.

Virtual Presents

`http://www.virtualpresents.com`

Photos of everything from cars, planes, and jewelry to sundry items such as tools can be virtually sent via photo postcard by Virtual Presents (see Figure 7.6). The site also features a selection of antique cards as well.

Figure 7.6

In addition to sending postcards of everyday objects, Virtual Presents also features a selection of lovely antique virtual cards.

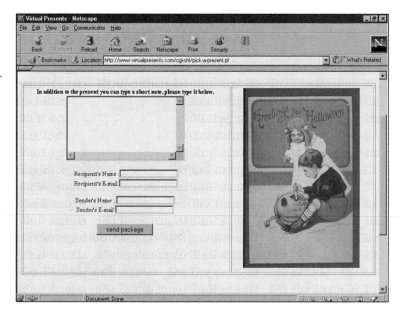

Love Notes

`http://www.loveandsex.com/nair/index.html?stuff=/cards/index`

Carter-Wallace, Inc., the makers of Nair, the hair removal product, have put together a selection of cards featuring animation. Filed under three broad categories (Love & Fun, Difficult Times, and Family) the cards are colorful and funky.

Dumbentia Internet Postcards

`http://www.dumbentia.com/postcards.html`

Dumbentia offers a small selection of original humorous cards as well as a library of more than 1,000 picture cards for all occasions. The cards come with many amenities, but for those who like to plan, the best feature might be the ability to schedule as far as three months in advance the day the card's notification message gets delivered.

She Was Two Different Women

I started to explore meeting women online because I'm somewhat isolated working from home as I do, and as I've gotten older, I've found it harder to meet people. Anyway, I met Mary through a personal ad and we started chatting online. We sent instant messages. We exchanged photos. She was quite the honey.

When we met, though, she seemed rather distant. Now I didn't expect there to be instant chemistry, but we had been corresponding for almost a month and I thought we had hit it off pretty well when we were online. The date ended in that no man's land between "She seemed nice" and "Was that the same person I had just spent a month getting to know?" When we chatted online the next day, she was her old self, free and easy. I felt like I was dating two women.

This pattern continued for the next few dates. Distant in person, warm online. I didn't know what to do. On our fourth date, she told me she had an admission to make. Here it comes, I thought. She's married. Or has a boyfriend. Or worse, a terminal disease. She told me she couldn't have kids. Evidently, I had put in my personal ad that I wanted children and she thought she would be rejected by me if I found out she was infertile.

Needless to say, they have a word for solving problems like ours: adoption.

—David

The Least You Need to Know

➤ If you have a crush on someone, let the Web help you make your feelings known without fear of immediate rejection.

➤ There are dozens of ways to woo another online including sending poetry, jokes, and kisses via email.

➤ If all else fails, sending an electronic postcard is a time-honored method of courting online.

Chapter 8

Advice IS Cheap!

In This Chapter

➤ Great places to get serious advice to all manner of relationship and dating questions

➤ Fun Web sites that offer humorous advice and parody the Web sites that give serious counsel

---

Who Are These People?

If this were the fifth century, you might seek advice from the wizened old hag who lives in the cloven wood. (The angels had touched her while still in her mother's womb and she has knowledge not of this realm.) Or, had you the means and access, you might have approached the wizard, who after consulting the oracle, would have been able to solve pretty much any problem. But today anyone, with or without a wizard's certificate, can set up shop on the Internet and dispense advice. Sure enough, some of these soothsayers have advanced degrees, toil as social workers, or command loyal national audiences who've come to rely on their insights. But only you can decide if the adviser's style and approach to relationship problems is right for you. Fortunately, there is a wide selection of advice Web sites to choose from and more being launched every month. Perhaps by the time you read this, even the Oracle will have one.

Serious Advice

Some soothe while they give advice. Others entertain. And still others just go about the business of giving counsel. But regardless of style, all the columnists mentioned in this section are giving their opinion in the fervent hope of solving your problem. So you can get a sense of each writer's style, a small quote from each Web site has been included. Please note that these samples are, for the most part, sub-sections of larger advice columns.

eMale

`http://womenswire.com/emale`

To whom can a woman with a relationship problem turn? Look no further than Andy Erdman, also known as eMale (see Figure 8.1). Representing the lone Y-chromosomed advice columnist for Women's Wire, a site dedicated to dispersing news and advice to its female constituency, eMale gives out lighthearted but incisive counsel on all interpersonal issues of the heart.

Figure 8.1

Andy Erdman, aka eMale, dispenses his online advice for Women's Wire.

Sample Advice from eMale

For four months a woman wanted to get to know a male acquaintance better, but both parties were too shy to start a conversation. eMale advised her:

"For many of us, there are few things harder than making "first contact." It's right up there with making four pancakes last through an entire dish of moo-shu pork. Or clearing your mind of the image of your grandparents having sex.

"So much is on the line, or so it seems: Will the other person like you? Will you look like a jerk? Will your little "drooling problem" flare up?

"But I ask you: Are any of these anxieties worth the regret of never having known [what might have been]?"

Delilah

`http://www.thriveonline.com/sex/experts/delilah/delilah.today.html`

Deb Levine, known to Web surfers as Delilah, has been giving out online advice on relationships and sexuality for more than five years (see Figure 8.2). The author of the book *The Joy of Cybersex*, Delilah uses her background in health education and social work to proffer even-handed assistance. Though she never pulls her punches, Delilah 's approach is enlightened and gentle.

Delilah

Figure 8.2

Deb Levine, author of The Joy of Cybersex, *serves up online advice as Delilah.*

Sample Advice from Delilah

A man who recently broke off an engagement to be married has met a woman online and thinks he is falling in love with her, though they have never met in person. He wonders if they have a future that could possibly involve marriage. Delilah advised him:

"Instead of rushing into things, give yourself some time to heal from the breakup with your fiancée. Reflect on what went wrong specifically—not just "it didn't work out." Make sure that you have your priorities in order before you enter into a new relationship.

"As for your online love, let her know that you care for her and are looking forward to meeting her in real life, but that it would be wise for both of you to take things slower and cool down a bit. That way, if you meet and there isn't a physical spark, you can still remain friends and possibly soulmates, without making a lifelong commitment to each other that you can't keep."

The Doc Is In

`http://underwire.msn.com/underwire/itspersonal/doc/doc.asp`

The titular doc in question is Dr. Joy Davidson, a psychotherapist from Seattle, who is known for a home video series titled "Secrets of Making Love to the Same Person Forever." Always careful to address the feelings of those who write to her, Dr. Davidson tends to tackle interpersonal problems of a fairly serious nature.

Sample Advice from Dr. Davidson

A divorced, single mother has gotten pregnant via an affair with a married man. He wants her to have the baby, but she's not sure what to do. Dr. Davidson advised her:

> "I understand your dilemma and your pain. But the issue you're facing is so serious that I need to say something to you in very strong terms. Please do not ever, EVER make a major decision about your future or that of a child based on promises, hopes, or dreams related to an affair with a married man.

> "A married man is NOT your partner. He may never be your partner despite his words or intentions to the contrary. Yes, he is your lover, but his commitment and primary involvement remain elsewhere. In considering whether to have this child, you must focus on your own values and feelings, not on him or your future together.

> "…Obviously, I cannot tell you what is "right." But I can tell you what I feel is wrong. It is wrong to be faithful to any but your own instincts and deeply held beliefs. It is wrong to deny the urgings of your own heart—no matter where they lead."

Ask Dr. Tracy

`http://www.loveadvice.com`

Dr. Tracy Cabot, with a Ph.D. in psychology, not only dispenses advice on the Web, but has written five books on relationships as well (see Figure 8.3). In addition to answering questions from readers, Dr. Cabot's site also maintains a "Love Library": archived articles of advice addressing common relationship problems that people often encounter. Her advice is straightforward and to the point.

"You've Got Mail" Redux

I am a 39 year-old man who, at the time of this story, was recently divorced. I live on the upper-west side of Manhattan, and two summers ago I met a woman online one Friday night. We clearly hit it off, so, as we both lived near each other, we decided to meet face to face the following Monday. Although this took place long before the release of the film "You've Got Mail," in which Tom Hanks romances Meg Ryan online, our romance followed an eerie parallel.

For our first date, we met at the 91st St. Community Garden where Hanks and Ryan also learn each other's true identity. Our second date (which was actually later the same day as my new acquaintance had made dinner plans with other friends as a polite way out in case I was a creep) took place at Cafe Lalo, where Meg Ryan waited fruitlessly (or so she thought) for her mystery man. Our third, and some of our subsequent dates, also paralleled locations from the film.

For those who don't believe what they see in the movies, "You've Got Mail" is an example of Hollywood fiction imitating Manhattan life. But the strangest irony in my finding love online was that my ex-wife left me for someone she had met in the same way.

—Jack

Figure 8.3

In addition to giving advice online, Dr. Tracy Cabot has written five books on relationships.

Sample Advice from Dr. Tracy

A man is in a relationship with a woman who is unsatisfied with everything about him. She mistreats him and he is confused about how to make the relationship work. Dr. Tracy Cabot advised him:

"If the woman you are dating is not satisfied with anything about you, why do you hang around? You've been having trouble with this relationship for between five and ten years. What on earth makes you think it's going to get any better at this late date?

"Relationships are like business deals. They either get better or they get worse, and once they've started in that downward spiral, it's almost impossible to turn them around. You've been in a downward spiral with this woman for so long, I doubt if it can turn itself around.

"If she says she can't be with a man like you, tell her fine, you can't be with a woman who puts you down...and mean it. You've been trying to make this relationship work for too long. It's time to find someone who will appreciate you."

Ask Dr. Love

http://www.askdrlove.com

Another psychologist now treading the online advice highway, Dr. Love is the pseudonym for Dr. Jamie Turndorf (see Figure 8.4). Each week Dr. Love answers three questions in the "Relationship Advice" section of her Web site, which also features answers to questions on sex and sexuality as well as articles on alternative health treatments. One of the nice features of the site is a searchable database of past relationship questions. In this way, you can search for articles on any relationship topic and read what the doctor has already written on the subject. Dr. Love, like the previous advice columnists mentioned, deals compassionately and directly with the issues she writes about.

Figure 8.4

Dr. Jamie Turndorf, aka Dr. Love, answers questions each week on her Web site.

Sample Advice from Dr. Love

A woman, engaged to be married, is worried that her sex drive is incompatible with her fiancé's. When he wants to make love, she feels his aggressive manner puts her off. Dr. Love advised her:

"You asked me to help you find a way to convey to your boyfriend that if he would only back off, you would come to him. Unfortunately, getting your boyfriend to back-off (not ask for sex) is not a solution to the problem, for several reasons.

"First, in a healthy relationship, both partners need to feel free to communicate their needs, sexual and otherwise. So, to tell your boyfriend to sit on his needs (no pun intended) would be placing him in a straitjacket. Even if we could convince him to do this, he will surely come to resent you for it, which will harm your relationship in the long run.

"What your boyfriend needs to work on is learning how to communicate his desire for you in a way that doesn't feel so aggressive to you. In other words, he must be true to his own inner needs, while being considerate of your feelings when he does approach.

"As for you, you need to focus on understanding why you feel so resentful when your partner asks you for sex when you aren't in the mood."

Dr. Love then went on to explore the dynamic of this relationship in great detail.

Ask-a-Chick

`http://ask-a-chick.com`

Although it is very clearly labeled as a nonprofessional advice site for entertainment purposes only, Ask-a-Chick answers an amazing range of questions with succinct aplomb (see Figure 8.5). Unlike other sites that usually answer one to five questions per week, it is not unusual for Ask-a-Chick to answer ten questions in a single day. Questions are answered anonymously by "a group of several chicks," and they maintain a library of several thousand previous questions categorized by topic.

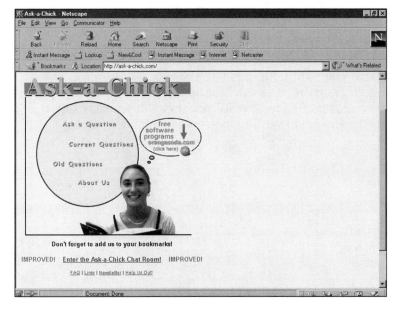

Figure 8.5

The Ask-a-Chick site handles an amazing volume of questions.

Sample Advice from Ask-a-Chick

A woman who is good friends with a couple having relationship problems has been told independently by both halves that each wants to leave the relationship. She wants to help them, but doesn't know what to do. Ask-a-Chick advised her:

> "You get them both together and sit them down and tell them 'you have both confided in me with problems that you are having in this relationship. You are now both together and I think it fair that you now discuss it between yourselves and come to some resolution and leave me out of it. I need to do this because you are both my friends.' Then simply take your leave or stay if they want you to. Simply tell them that you won't be a referee."

Flirt

http://www.flirt.com/advice/index.html

The guiding powers behind Flirt realize that different people prefer their advice from different sources. As such they have four advice columnists, each devoted to a separate segment of the online population. Brigitte and Michael answer relationship questions for the general community as well as those who specifically seek a male or female perspective. There's also Angel, who has a masters degree in psychology and specializes in giving advice on flirting, especially to those over 40. And finally there's Eve who, with a masters in counseling psychology, specializes in conflict resolution. All four of these columnists proffer serious advice to their readers, each from a unique perspective.

Sample Advice from Michael of Flirt

A woman has a platonic relationship with a man who wants to remain "just friends," but she wants something more. She wants to know what she can do. Michael advised her:

> "I know this isn't what you want to hear, but all I can suggest is wait. Wait to see if things change. If you try to press the issue you would most likely push him away. If he does actually have feelings for you they will probably surface, eventually. Meanwhile, you might want to look toward brighter horizons."

I'm Nobody, Who Are You?

I didn't meet my boyfriend online. We actually met in person when a mutual friend introduced us. I thought he was pretty cute, but we were both so shy that neither of us did much that first meeting other than smile politely and make small talk. Two months passed and I had already forgotten the disappointment of that evening when I received an email from him. It said, "I was wondering if it would be OK if I wrote to you from time to time." I wrote back, "Only if I'm allowed to reply."

What followed was the blossoming of two exceptionally introverted people discovering each other online. Starting as a trickle of email, we progressed to instant messaging, and then to private online chatting. We probably waited too long before we actually spoke on the telephone (almost another two months), but once we did, our relationship flourished into the real world. We have been dating face to face now for almost six months. Had it not been for the Internet, I might not have been allowed to discover this man who I plan to spend my entire life with.

—*Kelly*

Not So Serious Advice

Many "so-called" advice columns on the Web are actually parodies of the real thing. Either dispensing outlandish advice or espousing a distinctly skewed view of the relationship landscape, these columns are often excellent entertainment, but if you follow the actual advice given, you'll probably need accredited psychological assistance in due time.

Self Help with Lori

`http://www.chickenhead.com/selfhelp/index.html`

Some of Lori's readers taunt her with silly questions. Angry questions. Questions that most mothers would just roll their eyes at while arranging for their child to enter the military academy. The great majority though, seem to pose serious questions. In either case, Lori couldn't care less, for she serves all with equal-opportunity mocking. An extremely funny, if sometimes shockingly rude site, Self Help with Lori (see Figure 8.6) follows through on its mission statement of helping the reader to "realize full-fledged positive peachiness!"

Figure 8.6

Lori not only listens to your troubles, but also to those of mollusks!

The Advice Lady

`http://www.size-eight.com/dating_advice.html`

Take an idealized 1950s view of dating, add in five marriages, throw out any comprehension of how people actually behave, and you've got The Advice Lady (see Figure 8.7). Though she means well, hers is a world populated by beliefs such as "The way to a man's heart is trout fishing." and "Don't ask a man out. He might mistake you for a harlot!" In all fairness, I should say I am partial to this site not only for its odd take on giving the worst possible, well-meaning advice, but also because I founded the company that publishes it.

Figure 8.7

Who is The Advice Lady? Only this cryptic illustration accompanies her column.

Brenda's Dating Advice for Geeks

`http://home.earthlink.net/~brendar`

Where does Brenda Ross find the time? Not only does she run About.com's fine Dating Advice site (see Chapter 5, "Do You Type Here Often?") and answer questions as Brigitte for Flirt's advice page, but also let's her hair down for the edgy Dating Advice for Geeks (see Figure 8.8). The site features links to other advice pages with columnists who give faux advice under such names as Mr. Bad Advice and Evil Ed, but the real gems lie behind a link called "You Asked for It." That page leads to Brenda's two advice columns ("Just Ask Brenda" and "Ask Brenda/Ask Ed") where she warns her readers "...I do appreciate all of your letters, but let me just warn you, if you send me a letter, I'm just going to make fun of it. I can't resist!"

Tips for Dating Emotional Cripples

`http://www.grrl.com/bipolar.html`

Although Tips for Dating Emotional Cripples (see Figure 8.9) does not offer advice to readers questions, it contains Web pages with insights to dating various types of men ranging from stoners to artists to The President of the United States. Having never dated a man, I can not vouch for the veracity of these tips, however they seem to range from the wacky to the dead-on. I especially liked this tip for dating a Goth boy: "Beware of the boy who thinks he can communicate with ravens and crows just because he saw the movie *The Crow* sixty times. This type also may dress like the Crow character (Eric Draven) until you remind him that a professional wrestler dresses the same way."

Figure 8.8

Is this the face of some-one who would make fun of you? You'd better believe it.

Figure 8.9

Tips for Dating Emotional Cripples features a wide variety of cripples to choose from.

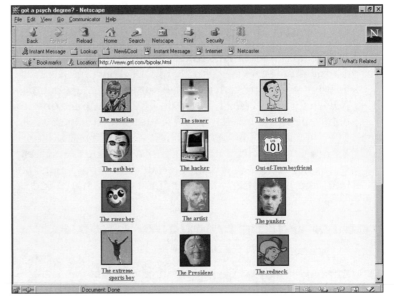

Dear Duke

http://members.home.net/dearduke/advice

Duke talks of relationships. Duke talks of philosophy. Duke talks about issues concerning life and death. However, no matter how many questions Dear Duke answers, you can rest assured that none of his responses are meant to be taken seriously.

Dear Toadmeister

`http://members.aol.com/TWSprockit/ask.html`

If, given a choice between Dear Duke and Dear Toadmeister, you had to guess which would be the more serious Web site, which would you pick? Believe it or not, the distinction belongs to Dear Toadmeister. Whereas Dear Duke makes no attempt whatsoever to answer questions earnestly, Dear Toadmeister actually has a mix of the silly, the humorous, and the serious.

The Least You Need to Know

➤ There are many good sources of advice for relationship and dating questions online. These Web advisers range from lay people to psychotherapists.

➤ Many sites that appear to give advice are actually parodies of the genre and are not meant to help people in any way other than to entertain.

Part 3
I Just Want Someone
I Can Talk To

Talking with someone via your computer has become so popular that this part of the book is devoted to that topic. We'll begin by exploring online chat and answering some common questions such as "How safe is it?", "What do I talk about?", and "What is cybersex?" We'll then take a look at Web sites that let you chat using words, pictures, video, or a combination of media. Next, we'll branch out to explore instant messaging (a form of communication that lets you track when friends are online) as well as newsgroups and message boards (public bulletin boards that allow group discussions). Finally, we'll investigate some ways to meet people online that most might not consider, as well as sites designed to plan your nuptials should you meet someone and want to make the arrangement permanent.

Chapter 9

I'm Typing As Fast As I Can

In This Chapter

➤ Why people chat online

➤ Safety tips to keep in mind while chatting

➤ A discussion of cybersex and the emotional ramifications of chatting online

➤ What people talk about when they meet for the first time

Chat and the Newcomer

To people who have never experienced online chat, talking with strangers by typing and reading one's conversation via the Internet might seem like a strange idea. Yet at one time so did the telephone. In fact, it was not too long ago that people thought email was just a waste of time and now it has become one of the most innovative tools of the twentieth century.

As with any relatively new technology, newcomers will have questions. This chapter will attempt to answer some of them. For those of you who already feel comfortable with online chat, skip ahead to Chapter 10, "Why Is Everyone Talking About Medieval Cookware?" where we'll learn about the choices in chat environments provided by the Web as well as other chat technologies. But for the person new to online chat, let's explore some fears and common misconceptions surrounding this way of communicating.

Is Chat Just Talking?

What's the big deal about talking to someone? I just open my door, walk down the street, and say hello to my neighbor. Or if I'm really desperate, I pick up the phone and call someone. I don't need my computer to have a conversation.

The above sentiment, although common, misses the point of online chat entirely: It's not talking to just someone, it's talking to the person or persons you *want* to talk to. Interested in forensics? Crafts? People your own age? All these and thousands of other topics are discussed daily in chat rooms geared around a shared interest, general populace, or specific area (see Figure 9.1). People flirt, develop feelings for each other, and fall in love online. They also argue, lie, manipulate, and generally act badly. Online chat presents the full range of possibilities inherent in any face-to-face conversation ranging from indifference to lust and back again to livid anger.

Figure 9.1

People flock to online chat rooms to find others who share their interests or background as this partial listing of the chat rooms available from Yahoo! Chat (http://chat. yahoo.com) *shows.*

And this is what people want? To talk to strangers?

Actually, no. What people want is connection. They hope to meet others online for friendship, love, sex, the basic trading of information, and to ease their loneliness. Some people express these needs in antisocial ways, but the vast majority of the online community is law-abiding and respectful.

Still, I tried chat once and it seemed like there were 30 people talking at once with at least that many conversations already started. It looked to me like gobbledygook.

Online chat can be confusing at first to the uninitiated, but usually, in a relatively short time, it becomes clear. Most chat environments have a main window where conversation takes place, each piece of dialogue being identified by the handle of the person who typed it. In addition there is usually also a list of all the people currently taking part in the conversation. All this, as well as other software functions available during online chatting, will be discussed in Chapter 10, "Why Is Everyone Talking About Medieval Cookware?"

As to the problem of entering a chat room while dozens of conversations are already in progress, that, unfortunately, is the nature of the online beast. Two things though might ease your mind. First, I recommend that people new to online chat frequent rooms specifically formed for helping chat rookies. This will give you the opportunity to get familiar with the software, environment, and peculiarities of this form of communication with others who are also learning. Not only will you be in a supportive atmosphere, but it's an excellent way to meet people in and of itself.

The second thing to keep in mind is that after you become facile with online chat, you will find yourself returning to the same rooms again and again. As this happens, you might find you've become part of an online community where you're familiar with the topics of conversation and its particular inhabitants. After this happens, you might be amazed to discover that even though you've entered into the middle of 12 conversations, you have a fairly good idea of what is going on.

Thank You, Cyberville

It was one of those small-world, synchronous, fateful things. Last summer I went to a baseball game with my friend Rich (a guy I went out with briefly a few years ago, whom I had met through the personals—you know, the old-fashioned newspaper ones) and his friend Sam. It was kind of a fix-up. That is, Rich planted the idea in my mind but not in Sam's. Less awkward that way.

At one point during the day, the topic of dating inevitably came up and Rich and Sam both talked about placing personal ads online—handle names, headlines, and all. I told them I had never done that. What I didn't tell them, and I don't really know why, is that I had just started writing my own profile to put online sometime soon. Maybe it was apprehension about using this kind of a service that kept me closed-mouthed, or maybe a teensy bit of shame. I'm not sure.

Overall, the afternoon was comfortable and fun. As for Sam, he had a lot of that right stuff to hook me in. He was easy to talk to, funny, and smart, and hinted at a seriousness and depth that was equally appealing. Whether or not he and I were a match with a capital "M" I couldn't be sure, but I had decided that if he called, I'd certainly go out with him.

He didn't call.

However, as planned, I put my profile online later that week. And who should be among my first five respondents, and undoubtedly the funniest, but Sam. Although he didn't know it was me, I recognized him from his unique headline and handle—something about tap-dancing monkeys and midgets. What made it especially fated was that even though the Web site that listed our personal ads had suggested plenty of matches for me, Sam's ad wasn't one of them. He told me later that he found my ad by browsing randomly.

At that point, I figured we were meant to go out at least once. We ended up going out more than once, but unfortunately, the relationship didn't last. We did have a couple of sweet, fun months together, though, and I am grateful to cyberville for bringing us together.

—Felicity

How Safe Is Online Chat?

I read all the time in newspapers and see on television stories about married men and women having affairs online and people being taken advantage of in numerous physical and psychological ways. There certainly seems to be a lot of sickos out there.

Unfortunately, there are disturbed people everywhere. The guy or gal you meet at a bar or at a party could as easily have a yen for vivisection as someone you meet online, but the same rule for socializing in both places remains in effect: Use your instincts. In addition, Chapter 3, "Was George Orwell Paranoid or an Optimist?" of this book lists many precautionary steps you can take while socializing online in a chat room. Some others that you might want to take note of are:

➤ Be aware of the purpose of the chat room you're in. Some chat environments are designed to let people explore alternative lifestyles. For instance, if the chat room is called "Sex on the Side" and you are not interested in dating a married person, you're in the wrong place.

➤ When you first enter a chat room, you might want to just listen to conversations already going on and get a feel for what the people are like before you start engaging them. Some chat rooms are very friendly (especially newbie chat rooms—those designed for people new to chat), but others are populated by people who've established online relationships that have been ongoing for years. In the latter case, you might be interpreted as a party crasher, rather than someone looking to meet new friends, if you barge into a conversation in progress.

➤ Although Chapter 3 dealt in detail with choosing the handle—or pseudonymous name—you choose to be known as while online, there is one more consideration when choosing a chat handle. Unlike a handle for a personal ad, there is no additional text identifying your gender to the rest of the chat room. If your goals include meeting people of the same or opposite sex, your handle should reflect this. Some women and men, however, prefer a gender-neutral handle to avoid sexual provocation or choose a handle of the opposite gender to have the experience of impersonating another's sex.

➤ Both women and men should be careful about being overtly sexual to total strangers. Unless you're looking for cybersex, predators are often very good at sensing the desire for sex and using it for their own purposes. This is also true of people who are overtly lonely or desperate for attention.

What's All This I Hear About Cybersex?

I keep hearing about this cybersex you just mentioned, but to tell you the truth, I have no idea what it is. How does it take place in a room full of chatting people?

When you meet someone for the first time in a chat room, it is usually in a public room—one that people throughout the Internet can join or leave at any time. After conversing for a while, you might ask this person (or be asked) to continue the conversation in a private room—a chat environment that only the people you invite can participate in (see Figure 9.2). Most cybersex takes place in private chat rooms, outside the watchful eyes of the general online community.

Figure 9.2

Most chat environments allow users to create or enter a private room for discreet discussion. Please note that this dialog box is not a standardized private room login box, and that the screen for entering/ creating a private room in the chat Web site or software you use might look different.

Cybersex during a chat session is the process whereby two (or sometimes more) people describe for each other all manner of sexual activity they would enact if actually present with the other person. A typical cybersex scenario might begin with someone describing his or her appearance, including descriptions of one's face, body, clothing, perfume/cologne, and expression. Foreplay might then ensue with one partner asking (or sometimes telling) how the other would like to be pleasured. This is then followed by one partner describing for the other, step by step, how he or she would perform a particular sexual act. After the cybersex act is completed (often with the person who received it achieving nonvirtual orgasm), the partners switch roles with the person who has received cybersex returning the favor to the one who just gave it.

Lastly, cybersex usually knows no bounds other than those placed by the people involved. It is not uncommon for the sex portrayed to involve descriptions of the surroundings the virtual sex is taking place in. Objects appear at the typing of a few chosen words and fantasies are fulfilled that might be beyond what someone would actually enact in his or her offline existence. Anything that stimulates the fantasy life of you and your partner in cybersex is okay as long as both parties are getting pleasure from the experience.

What if I don't want to have cybersex? Do I have to participate?

Absolutely not. In fact, the overwhelming majority of online chatting interactions have nothing to do with cybersex.

Not a Substitute

I met "Carl" over Christmas break while I was visiting from college. I was online when, like usual, I got an instant message from a complete stranger. He asked whether I had a picture and I told him that I was using my parents' computer at home and didn't have my picture on it. No response. After about five minutes, I blew up. I was sick of people asking for a picture and ignoring me if I didn't send one. So, I took it out on him in a nasty instant message that I knew would appear immediately on his computer. He apologized, said he didn't mean to ignore me, and, in this way, we began our online relationship.

We continued emailing the rest of the break (he went to the same state university I attend). After a week or so of being up at college, we chatted online again, and discussed meeting. We soon found that we lived in dorms right next to each other and that he was rooming with somebody whom I attended high school with. We soon started dating in person.

When summer came, Carl and I kept talking online every night, but we were physically apart. I felt that only talking online made the relationship difficult. You lose the humanity in a conversation. You are forced to rely entirely on words, no facial expressions, no body language, no tone of voice to guide you. I have no problem dating someone online—I'd do it again—but after the relationship is started, at a certain point, there has to be some actual contact away from the computer.

—*Millie*

Then what would I talk about? I'm afraid I wouldn't have anything to say.

This is one of the most common fears people have before venturing online to chat. "What do I say? People will think I'm boring. What if I have a typo? Then people will think I'm stupid and boring." But what you've got to realize is that people are looking to meet you as much as you're looking to meet them and they have all the same fears you do. As such, many conversations start with basic information: What state do you live in, what do you do for a living, what hobbies do you enjoy, and so on. After you find common ground with someone, chatting with them online will become easier. In the event someone mocks or insults you, just leave the conversation. Remember, the whole purpose of chatting online is to find people you want to talk to. As for typos during an online chat, they are fairly common and people usually overlook them.

But don't people in chat rooms have strange symbols and abbreviations that they use instead of English?

You're referring to acronyms and emoticons—the former being a word formed from the initial letters of each word of a phrase (for example, ASAP meaning As Soon As Possible) and the latter being a small picture created from keyboard symbols which is usually used to suggest an emotion or action. These are discussed in detail in Chapter 4, "Is That Email in Your Inbox or Are You Just Happy to Read Me?"

However, online chat has developed its own slang with some words having several variations in meaning. If someone uses a term you're not familiar with, just ask for a definition. Many people online are happy to share their knowledge. Following are a few common online chat expressions:

Chat Expression	Definition
Nick	Short for nickname or handle.
go private	Join me in a private chat room.
to cyber	Join me for cybersex.
IM or PM	Instant message or private message. Many chat environments enable you to send a private message to another while still in a public chat room. Sometimes also referred to as a "whisper."
Kick or kicked	Often refers to having been kicked out of a chat room, usually for bad behavior toward others.

Does Online Chatting Take an Emotional Toll?

Let's say I meet someone in a chat room who I think is really terrific. How do I know they are who they say they are? And what about the emotional end of online chatting? I hear people can fall in love or even get addicted to having cyber-relationships.

The fact is you can never be sure someone is telling you the truth until the passage of time has proven that person reliable or not. However, if you review the Guidelines for Keeping Yourself Safe in Chapter 3 ("Was George Orwell Paranoid or an Optimist?"), you'll be able to spot the obvious signs of people being less than truthful.

As for your emotional well-being while online, only you can monitor that. People fall in love online everyday. Sometimes it's just an infatuation. Sometimes people believe they are in love, but it is only the need to pacify a desperation that exists inside them. And sometimes people actually fall into a mature love that will last an entire lifetime.

Last, online chat addiction does indeed happen, although it is not the actual chatting that people get addicted to, but the emotional and mental stimulation they receive from it (see Figure 9.3). If your online chat life (and the amount of time you spend occupied in it) is interfering with your offline existence (for example, things such as your job, offline relationships, and day-to-day activities get neglected), then you need to seek professional help. The great majority of people who participate in online chat never become addicted, but do find it a pleasurable and entertaining component to their lives.

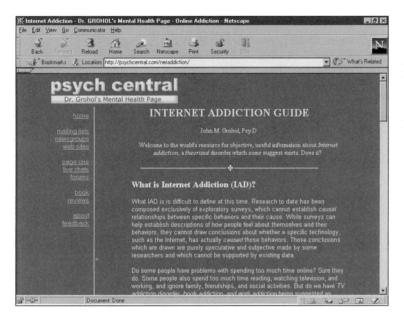

Figure 9.3

Not everyone believes people can get addicted to the Internet and interactive aspects of it, such as chat. The Internet Addiction Guide (`http://psychcentral.com/netaddiction`*) debates the issue and has links to many other Web sites concerned with the topic.*

I'm starting to look forward to getting online and chatting with people, but I'm not sure about what software to use.

Most online chatting discussed in this book will require only your Web browser. However, don't let the mechanics of what software you'll need to chat online concern you at this juncture. We'll explore the different types of available chatting environments in Chapter 10, "Why Is Everyone Talking About Medieval Cookware?"

One last question. I'm a little confused about America Online and chatting. Are they the same thing? How does the Internet fit into this equation?

America Online (AOL) is what is referred to as an online service. People who pay AOL a monthly fee get to use its proprietary software, which allows them to access features and services that AOL provides to its members. One of the things that makes AOL attractive to its clientele is the hundreds of chat rooms it provides. AOL members can access the Internet via AOL, but its chat rooms are not available to the Internet users who do not have AOL. As such, if you belong to AOL, you will have access to many of the chat rooms discussed in this book. If you connect to the Internet in some way other than AOL, you will have access to all the chat rooms we discuss. But because AOL's chat rooms are closed off to most of the Internet, this book will not discuss them.

The Least You Need to Know

➤ Although online chatting might be new to you, it is a common technology that millions enjoy. It can be used to put you in touch with people who share your interests.

➤ Take care to follow the same precautions outlined in Chapter 3 to keep yourself safe while chatting online. In addition, be sure you are in a chat subject area that you feel comfortable with.

➤ Although some people do have cybersexual relationships online, the vast majority of online discussions have nothing to do with sex and involve the scope of human discourse from the particulars of daily life to esoteric discussions of unique hobbies.

➤ Online chatters do have their own terminology, but much of it is discussed in this chapter and Chapter 4.

Chapter 10

Why Is Everyone Talking About Medieval Cookware?

If You're New to Chat

Traveling between chat environments is a little like traveling throughout Italy: Even though you might know Italian, regional dialects and slang might make communicating that much harder. And although you don't have to worry that your search for a restroom could be misinterpreted as a marriage proposal, each chat room has it's fair share of quirks, both interpersonal and technical.

If you're a chat neophyte, the best place to begin exploring online discussion is with Web-based text chat. Most Web-based chat requires no additional software other than your Web browser and knowledge of very few, if any, commands. There is though, one technical consideration you might need to be aware of: whether the Web-based chat you are using is utilizing HTML or Java (see Figure 10.1).

Figure 10.1

This table from Yahoo! Chat shows the browser requirements for using this particular Web-based chat environment.

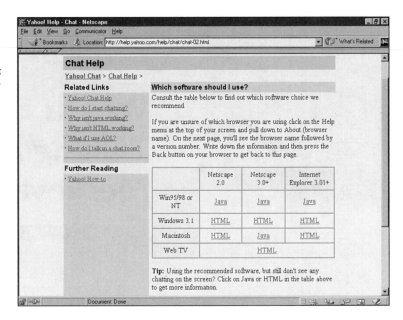

What Version Web Browser Do You Have?

Finding out what version of Netscape Communicator or Microsoft Internet Explorer you have is easy. In either program click the **Help** menu. In Communicator, click the **About Communicator** command or for Internet Explorer the **About Internet Explorer** command. Either will then display the information.

Without getting overly technical, HTML and Java are two programming languages used to allow Web sites to host chat rooms. Some Web sites that offer chat will present you with a choice of these two technologies prior to entering the chat environment. If your Web browsing software is several years old or you're using Windows 3.1, a Macintosh loaded with Internet Explorer, or WebTV, you'll probably need to use the older technology of HTML. If you are using Windows 95 or 98 and your version of Netscape Communicator or Microsoft Internet Explorer is less than a couple of years old (version 3.0 or higher for Communicator, version 3.01 or higher for Internet Explorer), then you should probably select Java. If you have the capability, selecting Java is the preferable choice because although both Java and HTML allow Web-based chat, Java, as the newer technology, is often faster and capable of offering more features. (In fact, some of the more recently launched chat sites only offer Java.)

There are exceptions to these guidelines, so in each case it doesn't hurt to check the Web site's chat room requirements before making your choice. Most Web sites post their browser requirements so users can make an informed decision (refer to Figure 10.1). However, if you do select Java and your browser requires HTML chat technology, often the only result is that you can't enter the chat room. (On occasion, selecting the wrong choice between HTML and Java might require you to relaunch your browser or restart your machine.)

Web-Based Text Chat

If there is one truism in online chat it is this: A chat room is only as good as the people it attracts. As such, the first two Web-based text chat sites that follow were selected because they attract large numbers of people and have established chat rooms dedicated to diverse subjects. In addition, they are great places for the beginner and the experienced chatter while offering a variety of chat features. The remaining Web-based text chat sites all provide a solid chat experience, but with one or more limitations. (All chat features discussed in this book are for the Java version of the Web site, where applicable.)

Yahoo! Chat

`http://chat.yahoo.com`

There is little wonder why Yahoo! Chat has become one of the largest Internet meccas for talking to people online (see Figure 10.2). In terms of features, ease of use, variety of chat rooms, and sheer volume of people chatting on the site, there is something for everyone. After you've signed up for a Yahoo! ID (if you haven't done so already to place a personal ad or open a free email account), the site brings you to an opening page where you can pick the chat room you want to participate in. Although a dozen or so choices are immediately available, clicking the **Complete Room List** link in the middle of the page will present you with an awe-inspiring choice of rooms. Besides environments catering to chatting in Spanish, French, English, and German, there are dozens of rooms devoted to particular television shows, movies, geographical locations, hobbies, romance, and lifestyle choices.

List of chat participants

Figure 10.2

The Yahoo! Chat environment is easy to use, yet boasts powerful features.

Conversation display window

Chat input box

Major chat tools (windows to the right change based on what is clicked here)

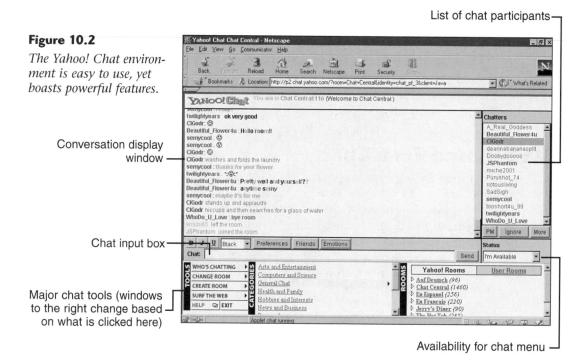

Availability for chat menu

Prior to entering a chat room, you'll probably want to read over your profile, an informational document that was created when you initially joined Yahoo! Chat. Your profile can disclose facets of your offline life, such as your name, age, and email address to others in a chat room. As such, Yahoo! Chat's main page provides a link to change your profile. In addition, you can create up to five additional profiles (or identities) that you can be known as within the chat rooms. After you've confirmed what profile information will be disclosed to other chat room participants, you're ready to start meeting people.

Yahoo! Chat's rooms are straightforward and easy to use. A list of all the people in the room is displayed on the right of the screen with a main chat window showing all dialogue from various parties. On the bottom of the chat window is a box to type your contribution to the conversation and, upon hitting your **Enter** key, it is labeled with your handle and sent for everyone else in the room to read.

Yahoo! Chat has many features that make the chatting experience fun. Double-clicking a chatter's name let's you send a private message or hold an entire discussion without the rest of the Internet listening in. Right click a chatter's name and you get a dialog box that will allow you to view his or her profile or add that person to a Friends list that will let you know each time you go online if your new acquaintance is already chatting in Yahoo! Chat. In addition, any emoticons you type during chat are displayed in the chat window as actual smiley-face pictures and an "emotions" command allows a chatter to send out prescribed third-person actions to the group (for example "handlename washes and folds the laundry"). All this and much more makes Yahoo! Chat a winner.

Language Unfit for a Sailor

Though many chat sites have filtering programs designed to stop obscene or salty language from being displayed in public chat rooms, those that use colorful phraseology are extremely clever at circumventing these security measures when they exist. As such, it is not uncommon for the occasional blue phrase to make its way into public chat discourse.

Excite Chat

`http://javatalk.excite.com/VP/java/gst_pickRoom.html`

Although it doesn't have all the bells and whistles of the Yahoo! Chat site, Excite Chat (see Figure 10.3) seems to have traded some amenities for sheer ease of use. This is immediately apparent at Excite Chat's sign-in screen. Although many chat sites require you to fill out a membership form prior to entering a chat room, Excite allows one to start meeting people after typing in a handle and choosing a chat room. The sign-in screen also offers the option of word filtering, a feature that will mask words Excite has designated obscene with #####. Although this cannot block double entendres and other innuendo, it does mask out the most obvious blue language. Though other chat sites including Yahoo! have similar filtering features, it's very much in line with Excite's ease-of-use mandate that this choice is one you make prior to entering its chat rooms.

Once inside the chat environment, Excite Chat provides a standard Web-based text chat room with a list of chat participants, a main chat window, and an input box to type your own contributions. So newcomers don't have to figure out what commands are available, big buttons at the bottom of the screen (see Figure 10.4) clearly display how users can perform common functions, such as changing chat rooms, sending an instant private message, or seeing what identity information a user has on file. Just highlight the user's handle in the chatter list, click a big button, and the Java script does what you ask (there is no HTML version).

Figure 10.3

Excite Chat's sign-in screen allows one to start chatting without providing a lot of information.

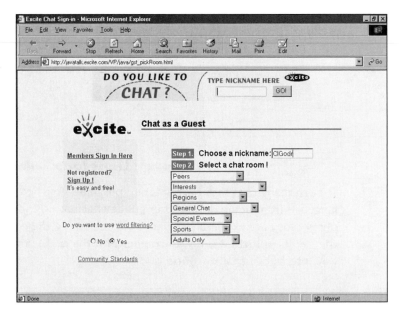

Figure 10.4

Large command buttons at the bottom of the Excite Chat environment make this an easy-to-use chat room.

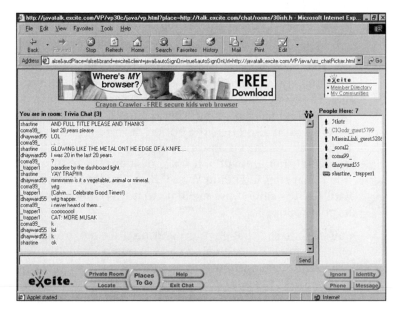

An especially nice Excite Chat feature for the newcomer is the clear placement of an Ignore button. Because it is impossible for chat sites to screen out those who would monopolize a room with profane or disruptive behavior, most feature an option to select a user on the list of chat participants and block that user's public or private messages from ever appearing onscreen. Though most sites offer this feature, Excite

Chat prominently displays its availability. Excite Chat did experience minor problems with Netscape Communicator 4.61 for Windows, specifically in displaying all the individuals in the list of chat participants, but overall it provides a solid chat experience.

Go Chat

http://www.go.com/Community

Technically, Go Chat is one of the best chatting environments on the Web (see Figure 10.5). The interface is clear, the few commands needed are clearly marked onscreen, and it works on all browsers flawlessly. But it needs to attract more people. Often the established chat rooms on the site are underpopulated or empty. Exacerbating this situation is the fact that because room population is not displayed prior to room selection, you often don't find out that a room is empty until you've traversed links to two or three pages. Fortunately, certain rooms, notably the coffeehouse and those arranged by age group or romantic predilection, have chatters regularly. In addition, just prior to this book going to press, Go Chat's owners acquired WBS Chat, an established Web-based chatting community with thousands of regular chat participants. If those chatters embrace the Go Chat site, as they most probably will, by the time you read this, the site should be swarming with people to meet.

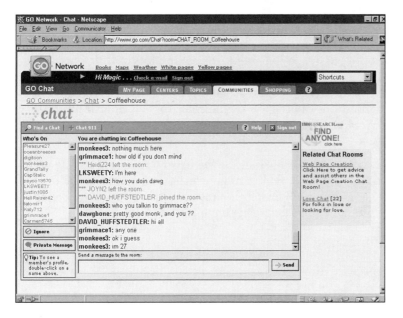

Figure 10.5

Go Chat provides one of the easiest to use chat interfaces on the Web.

Go Chat does require that users become a member of the site prior to using the chat rooms. Membership is free and does have privileges like no-cost email, Web page hosting and use of bulletin boards (see Chapter 12, "All the News That's Fit to Post"). There is no need to look for a separate link to sign up for membership, as you will be prompted to do so as soon as you try to enter a chat room. Although there are even less features than Excite Chat (for instance, private room creation did not exist as of this writing), it is the easiest chat system on the Web. Go Chat features a yellow tip area on its screen that posts useful suggestions to users and a clearly marked help link that when clicked pops up a window that can be read in five minutes and answers any questions you could have about using the chat facilities. As soon as more people learn about Go Chat, there is no doubt this will become one of the primo chatting destinations on the Web.

MSN Web Communities Chat

`http://communities.msn.com/chat`

If you are an experienced online chatter and use Microsoft Internet Explorer on a Windows machine, MSN (Microsoft Network) Web Communities Chat can offer a very good place to socialize online. If, however, you use another Web browser or operating system (that is Macintosh or Windows 3.1), you are shut out or, in some cases, only able to access the system by downloading special software. Though at press time Microsoft had posted a notice saying support for Macintosh and Windows 3.1 machines was planned for the future, no specific date was given.

Once registered with the site, MSN's Web-based text chat has lots of little quirks that might throw the chat newcomer for a loop. As such, Microsoft supplies a lengthy page of frequently asked questions at `http://communities.msn.com/chat/faq.asp`, which can answer such questions as how to exit the chat (there is no exit button—you just go to another Web page or close your browser) and what a whisper is (MSN's lingo for a private message).

Although MSN chat might present some issues for the new chatter or someone without the right software setup, it does provide a huge selection of chat rooms and a very large, ever-growing community of chatters to meet. For those willing to accept these limitations, MSN provides a solid chatting environment.

Lycos

`http://chat.lycos.com`

Lycos' chat is similar to many of the aforementioned chat environments. On the plus side it's easy to use, attracts a large community of chatters for you to meet, and provides a host of amenities including the creation of private rooms and the ability to pepper your chat dialogue with playful images you can select from a library it provides. On the minus side, it has problems working with Netscape Communicator, the site does not post advance counts detailing chat room population (causing the occasional entrance into an empty chat room), and all chat takes place in a pop-up window that, unfortunately, leaves less room for reading ongoing conversations than a chat room using a full computer screen. Still, Lycos has a loyal following among its chatters, and upon becoming a free member of its site, you can check it out for yourself.

IRC Web-Based Text Chat

Internet Relay Chat (IRC), the granddaddy of online chat systems, first came into existence in 1988 and has been used for text chatting by millions of people since. But with the advent of the Web, many Internet newcomers shied away from the technology due to the extra effort it required in learning special commands and acquiring downloadable chat software. However, in an evolutionary move, IRC and chat rooms that use IRC commands have become accessible via Web browsers. Although users can still experience IRC with special chat software, now the average Web surfer can explore many of these chat rooms as well—and, as an added bonus, can navigate the chat environment with knowledge of just a few of the technology's commands.

The following Web sites, as well as many of those you'll encounter when looking up new sites in the chat indexes mentioned later, are chat sites allowing easy access to IRC or Web-based chat sites using IRC commands. To navigate them, you'll need to know some IRC rules and commands.

IRC commands for Web pages always start with the forward slash (/) and are usually followed by additional information. For instance, to type a message to the entire chat room in IRC there would be no command; but to send a private message, you would begin the message with the command /msg followed by the person's handle (called a nickname in IRC lingo) and the actual text of the message. So in the example

```
/msg Happylady I really enjoyed chatting with you.
```

a private message reading "I really enjoyed chatting with you." would be sent to the chatter named Happylady.

Some other commands commonly used in IRC-based Web chat rooms are listed in the following table:

IRC Command/Variable	Explanation
/quit PartingComment	Exits a chat room and sends one final comment before leaving.
	Example:
	/quit Goodnight all!
	would send the message "Goodnight all!" and then exit the user from the room.
/me ThirdPersonComment	Allows a chatter to refer to himself in third person during a chat session.
	Example:
	/me looks across the chat room and notices Happylady.
	would send the chatter's nickname followed by the message that was typed. So if the above command was issued by the chatter named MoonDoggie, the chat room would read "MoonDoggie looks across the chat room and notices Happylady."
/help	Lists common commands available to the chatter in many IRC rooms.

There are many other commands, but fortunately, they're not often needed to enjoy the Web sites accessing IRC-based chat rooms. For those who'd like to learn more about IRC, there are many fine Web resources detailing its workings and the downloadable (and often free) software packages used to access its chat rooms. Some good places to find this information are:

IRChelp.org Internet Relay Chat (IRC) Help Archive

http://www.irchelp.org

New IRC Users.com

http://www.newircusers.com

mIRC's "What Is IRC?" Article

http://www.mirc.co.uk/irc.html

For those who would like to jump right into chatting with IRC commands, let's visit two of the more popular Web sites that host this type of chat.

Talk City

`http://www.talkcity.com`

If you know the /msg and /me commands, you're ready to use Talk City because all the other major IRC commands are neatly executed via an excellent Web interface that makes the site a joy. Often Web sites with names that suggest a huge panorama of offerings, fall far short of the suggested mark, but Talk City offers hundreds of chat rooms with thousands of chatters participating online at any given time.

It's clear Talk City was designed from the ground up with the chatter in mind. You can start chatting immediately without becoming a site member, but if you sign up for a free membership, you can register your chat handle so no one else but you can use it. Prior to entering a chat room, Talk City displays the number of current chatters already inside (see Figure 10.6) so that users don't get annoyed at having to pop from empty room to empty room looking for a discussion (although it must be noted there are rarely empty rooms at this site). After you are inside a room, chatting is speedy and efficient, though rooms can often have as many as 50 people, making for a raucous affair. In addition, private messages appear in the main chat window mixed in with the public messages, so you must be on the lookout for them as they can get lost in the group discussion.

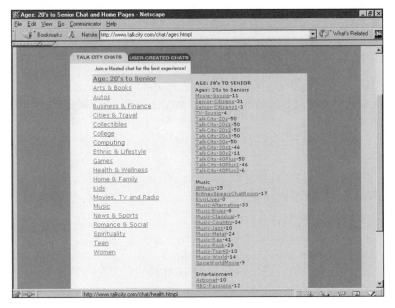

Figure 10.6

Prior to entering a Talk City chat room, chatters can see how many people are already in the room.

ChatSpace

http://community.chatspace.com

ChatSpace is an umbrella site, which supplies links to and hosts more than 650 individual chat sites. Most use IRC commands to varying degrees, but many provide Web page links and buttons for commands such as private messaging, ignoring chatters, and third-person actions. At the same time, knowing the few IRC commands discussed earlier is a godsend as using /quit to leave a chat room saves the inexperienced user from looking for an "exit" link where sometimes none exists. The chat rooms in ChatSpace vary widely in volume of chatters and quality of features, but the sheer magnitude will provide many appealing choices for a large swath of the online chatting population.

Chat Indices

For some, the previously listed sites will provide all the chat they ever need. But if you're curious about what other chat sites abound on the Web, a chat index is the perfect place to start.

The Ultimate Chatlist

http://www.chatlist.com

The Ultimate Chatlist (see Figure 10.7) divides the hundreds of sites it links to under general categories such as Business, Entertainment, and Home & Garden. Once on a category page, the sites are not in any discernable order, alphabetical or otherwise. However, the adventurous will find all manner of unusual chat rooms devoted to topics that range from home repairs to winning contests and sweepstakes. And if you're looking for a chat site on a particular topic (or by name), there's a chat search engine on the site's home page.

The WebArrow Chat Directory

http://www.webarrow.net/chatindex

Another general chat index, The WebArrow Chat Directory is not as extensive as the Ultimate Chatlist, but does have a List of Chats page that details oodles of chats in alphabetical order. As is the case for the Ultimate Chatlist, there are also sub-lists of chat sites organized by category.

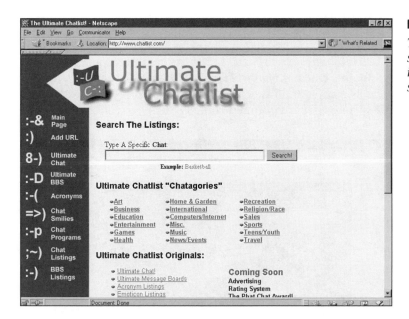

Figure 10.7

The Ultimate Chatlist's search engine makes finding the chat you want a snap.

RIC Language Chat Sites

`http://rivendel.com/~ric/resources/langchat.html`

A polyglot's dream, the RIC Language Chat Sites page offers up links to dozens of sites offering online chat in French, Spanish, German, Hebrew, Hindi, Arabic, and many other languages. In addition it offers links to three sites that allow multilingual chatting, some of which even do translation to English from other languages while you chat. The site might take a little while to load as all the links are on a single page, but if you're looking to stretch your language skills online, there's probably no better resource.

Graphical Chat

Though the great majority of online chatting is text-based, the last few years have seen the growth of graphical chat. In graphical chat, you still type your dialogue at the keyboard, but instead of it appearing onscreen surrounded by everyone else's words, it usually appears in a word balloon coming from a picture that represents you. These graphical stand-ins, often called avatars, represent all the other people in the chat room as well, so when viewing the screen one sees pictures talking to each other, as in a comic strip. Unlike comics though, one can move their avatar from room to room while enjoying (depending on the site) animation, sound, special effects, and high quality artwork, all of which enhance the chat experience. Needless to say, graphical chat can be a lot of fun.

OnChat

`http://www.onchat.com`

From an ease-of-use standpoint, OnChat is in a class by itself (see Figure 10.8). It needs no special software (as most graphical chat environments do), works with all browsers, and provides a speedy chat environment.

Figure 10.8

This treehouse is one of OnChat's many graphical chat environments.

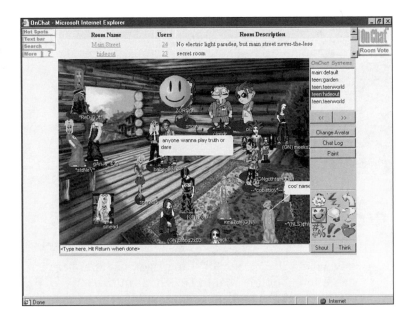

Logging onto the site is a breeze as chatters can converse immediately as a guest or register to become an OnChat member. Membership is free and allows you (among other things) to customize your avatar, have your own private chat room, and play with simple interactive objects (balls, postboxes, anvils, and so on) in the chat environment. After you're logged on, learning to use the graphical chat environment takes under five minutes.

Because the site has a frequent flow of traffic, there are always chatters to socialize with and a good selection of avatars for both members and guests to choose from. Chatters can talk privately or publicly and can punctuate their speech with colorful graphics (hearts, a light bulb, exclamation points, a question mark, and so on). A huge selection of nicely rendered environments (tree houses, gardens, a bookstore, a café, and so on) also add to the fun. All in all, OnChat strikes the right balance, remaining fun and functional while still supplying the bells and whistles one would expect from a graphical chat environment.

Across a Crowded Room

Online chat is weird. You can have 20 people ask you your gender and age and have them all abandon you within seconds when they find out you're not what they're looking for. At the same time you can go into a room and have a three-hour conversation with a bunch of total strangers pass in a flash. But it wasn't until I tried some visual chat rooms that I experienced a real, but really bizarre, connection.

I was represented in the room by a picture of a bullfrog dressed in a business suit. I thought it was pretty funny and in some ways resembled me. Connie's avatar was just a standard cartoon girl with hiking gear and a backpack. We hit it off almost immediately.

After a short while we continued our conversation in a private room. Now there's no cybersex in this story. Not even a whole lot of flirting. But as I'm talking to this woman who's actually hundreds of miles from me I'm watching our two cartoon characters. They're standing side by side. Holding hands. Maybe she's even resting her head on my shoulder. And as crazy as this sounds, as crazy as I feel writing this, I'm developing feelings for this girl in a backpack as we discuss movies, music, books, coffee, you name it. And I can't say for sure, but she's falling for this distinguished frog in a business suit.

We end up chatting until about 5:00 a.m. We exchange first names. Email addresses. Assurances that we are both single. We have a cyber-kiss, which amounts to nothing more than typing the word "Smooch" so it appears in a word balloon above our heads. Since then we have exchanged photos and talked on the phone. But three months later we still meet, almost weekly, a frog and a princess, holding hands in the darkness of cyberspace.

—Mel

The Palace

`http://www.thepalace.com`

There are two ways to socialize in The Palace's graphical chat environment: via the Palace Viewer or The Palace User Software, both available for download at the site. The Palace Viewer is a small piece of software that allows you to use your Web browser to chat graphically. However, using my 56K modem, I found it fairly slow.

Though downloading and installing The Palace User Software (free of charge and available for both Windows and Macintosh) is more time consuming, it provides the better chatting experience.

After The Palace User Software is downloaded and installed, the program offers an insane selection of features and commands. As such, a graphical chat site called The Practice Palace, which contains tutorials, is the best place for new Palace users to get their feet wet. After you're familiar with using the software and communicating with others, The Palace offers dozens of graphical chat sites based on media properties (including Star Wars, South Park, and The SciFi Channel) and varying locales such as a mansion and a rain forest (see Figure 10.9).

Figure 10.9

Feel free to graphically chat in The Palace's mansion bedroom.

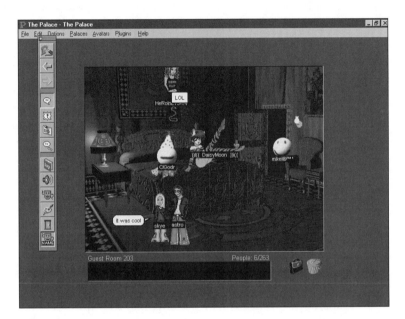

Features include the ability to download different avatars (or create your own); dress up your appearance with props (small graphic files that accessorize your avatar: glasses, hats, masks, shoes, jewelry, and so on); change the shape of your word balloon to emphasize emotional content; and send sound effects as well as text to the entire room or privately to individuals. Some Palace sites feature animation, sound, and even interactive games. All in all, if you have the time to learn to use its software and own a moderately fast computer system, The Palace could provide a great place to hang out.

Other Graphical Chat Sites

Should you feel a hankering to explore what other companies are doing with graphical chat, following are two sites that have their own approaches to the technology. Like The Palace, they require an expenditure of time for downloading software (or, in the case of Worlds Ultimate 3D Chat Plus, a CD-ROM is available for purchase), installation, and learning the graphical environment. They both offer various features and artwork to add to the chat experience and amuse the eye.

Worlds Ultimate 3D Chat Plus

http://www.worlds.net

Active Worlds

http://www.activeworlds.com

Video Chat

Video chat, though it has been around for years, has yet to gain wide acceptance. Part of the problem is its technical limitations. One needs special software, a video camera (usually a small one that's specially made to plug right into a computer), and patience while setting it up. In addition, the frame rate (the speed at which the video transmits over the Internet) is often slow, resulting in a choppy video transmission. Because sound is often transmitted (at varying quality), a good set of speakers and a microphone might also be useful. And finally, because there isn't a huge pool of people (relative to the text chat community) taking advantage of video chat, one often has to put effort into finding a fulfilling conversation. That being said, with the price of cameras and software going down (as of this writing some software was free and computer video cameras were being sold for under $100), the technology has become more affordable. So if you don't mind a technical challenge, have a relatively speedy modem and computer, and enjoy tinkering with technologies that, though fascinating, might require an investment in time spent learning them, then you might want to check out the following sites.

CU-SeeMe and CU-SeeMe Pro

http://www.wpine.com

Although White Pine, the company that manufactures CU-SeeMe for Windows and Macintosh, charges for their software, it is one of the easiest (if not the easiest) video chat software packages on the market in terms of both use and setup. Features such as being able to chat one-on-one or in groups of people as well as in color or black and white video, allow almost all types of video cameras and computer setups to work with the software. One especially nice feature is that you can connect to another person who is already online for a video chat if you know the other person's email address (many packages use a string of numbers called an IP or Internet Protocol address for this purpose). And, because White Pine is committed to being a one-stop shop for all your video chat needs, they sell combo packages of video cameras with their software.

Microsoft NetMeeting

`http://www.microsoft.com/windows/netmeeting`

The good news is Microsoft NetMeeting is free. The bad news is it's only made for Computers running Microsoft Windows and for one-on-one chatting. If you want to see the video of several people at once or meet strangers over the Internet, NetMeeting is not for you. However, if you are maintaining a relationship with one person who is far away, NetMeeting can provide a relatively inexpensive way to see that person while conversing. Microsoft recommends those who use NetMeeting have a Pentium 133MHz or faster computer and a 56K or faster modem.

CuSeeMe.net

`http://www.cuseeme.net`

Despite its name, CuSeeMe.net is *the* Internet site for information on all video chatting software and hardware, not just CU-SeeMe (see Figure 10.10). It provides links to manufacturers of video chatting and conferencing packages, as well as computer video camera manufacturers and personal Web sites created by people in love with the technology. There are also links to sites allowing you to download free versions of CU-SeeMe (it was originally developed at Cornell University) although installing this software could be a huge technical challenge for some, as it does not come with the installer program White Pine provides in the commercial version. This site is a great resource for anyone interested in video chat on the Internet.

Personal Ads Chat

Lastly, it should be mentioned that many of the personal ads sites discussed in Chapter 5, "Do You Type Here Often?" and Chapter 6, "I Want Values for My Money," have their own chat rooms devoted to helping their members meet others. If you've already posted a personal ad on one of those sites you might want to check out the other members by joining them in conversation.

Figure 10.10

CuSeeMe.net is the place to go to find links to information on Internet video chat.

The Least You Need to Know

➤ Web-based text chat is the best type of chat for newcomers to learn about online discussion.

➤ Internet Relay Chat, a forerunner of Web-based text chat, has evolved to a point where it can be accessed from the Web.

➤ Graphical chat, which allows people to have illustrations represent them online, can be a lot of fun.

➤ Video chat, although not widely accepted, is only practical for those with the right equipment and the patience to learn about the technology.

Chapter 11

The Velvet Rope

In This Chapter

➤ Learn what instant messaging is and what it can do to help you meet people online

➤ Explore different instant messaging software packages and find out which are more suited for beginners and which cater to advanced Internet users

➤ Learn which instant messengers offer additional features such as checking email and transmitting files

It's All in the Message

If only life offline were like instant messaging: You talk to only the people you want or to strangers depending on your mood; if you don't want to be disturbed, you can become invisible; and in the rare instance you are contacted by a person you find undesirable, you can stop that person from bothering you forever. Such are the powers of an Instant Messenger (IM), software that lets you track if any of your friends are online, and then send one (or more) a message that within seconds pops up on his or her screen. And, unlike most personal email, the message arrives without the recipient having to retrieve it. Because everyone has the power to keep tabs on others, privacy controls in most IMs allow you to choose who you will allow to monitor you.

Instant Messengers have become so widespread that the two most popular packages (ICQ and AOL Instant Messenger—both owned by America Online) boast a combined user population of more than 40 million. Unfortunately, as this book goes to press, no two instant messaging programs can communicate with each other. This means if you have ICQ and a friend has Yahoo! Messenger, you can not exchange correspondence, and if a third friend has a third package forget about that as well. The Internet Engineering Task Force (an independent group involved in the technical evolution of the Internet), as well as America Online, are both working on developing a method for all IM packages to communicate with each other. I believe, whether it is weeks, months, or years, it is just a matter of time before you can send an instant message and, just like email, regardless of the recipient's software, it will arrive at its destination. In the interim, if you are interested in communicating with particular people, find out what IM software they are using and download that (currently the ones listed in this chapter are all free). However, if you want to use instant messaging to meet new people, look through the choices that follow and pick the one that most appeals to you.

ICQ

http://www.icq.com

ICQ ("I Seek You") is the veritable all-purpose handyman of the instant messaging world (see Figure 11.1). Although it started out as a humble IM program, ICQ now boasts what it calls Services—mini programs that check your email, schedule alarm clock reminders for important appointments or tasks, keep to-do lists, and much more. Despite these impressive personal information tools, ICQ is still primarily used for instant communication using the Internet.

Figure 11.1

ICQ's simple mode screen notifies you when friends are online or off.

The ICQ contact list

Commands to switch to Advanced mode, find a chat partner, and other functions

Adds contact list names for tracking when friends are online and sending them

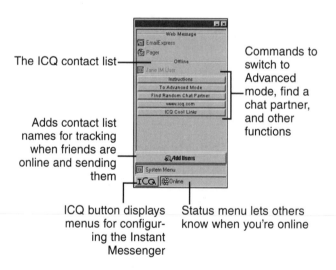

ICQ button displays menus for configuring the Instant Messenger

Status menu lets others know when you're online

Because the sheer volume of features in ICQ (see Figure 11.2) can be confusing to the newcomer, the software's developers have given the program two operational modes: simple and advanced. Advanced mode makes available ICQ's full functionality, and simple mode limits itself strictly to the program's most popular instant messaging features. In addition to such IM mainstays as maintaining a contact list of those you converse with; having the program notify you when people on your list are online; having the ability to send instant messages to those on and off your list; and being invisible (hiding your online presence to others), ICQ has some very nice features to put you in contact with those in the online community you've never met. Chief among these is the ability to find a random chat partner. Using categories such as General Chat, Romance, Students, Seeking Men, and Seeking Women, users can search out people currently online who have made themselves available for meeting new people. When the program finds a person, it displays a short profile revealing whatever personal information was submitted by the prospective chatter. You can then decide if you want to request a chat session, send them a short note, or search for someone else. Making yourself available to be contacted by random chatters is also easy to do, as is real-time chatting with anyone on your contact list.

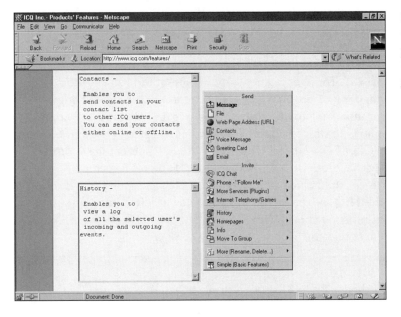

Figure 11.2

This ICQ menu displays just a few of the operations performed by the program.

ICQ also lets people find you by providing ways for those who don't use the program to send you instant messages. After you've downloaded and registered ICQ, the program provides you with a "Worldwide Pager on the Web," a Web page that anyone with a browser can access. Once there, a person can type their message onto the Web page, click the **Send Message** button, and if you are online, you'll get it immediately. If you're offline it will be waiting for you the next time you start ICQ (which can be configured to launch whenever you connect to the Internet). In addition, ICQ provides you with an email address that those without the program can use to send you an instant message. The correspondent sends you a regular email, but instead of going to an email account, it's routed directly to your screen when you're online or will be waiting for you when you log on. To let people know about these new ways to contact you, ICQ provides a form letter (which you can personalize) that you can email directly from the program to whomever you want.

ICQ Beeps and Boings

One of the best features (and sometimes one of the most frustrating) of ICQ is that you can customize how the program operates. Especially fun is the ability to change what sounds ICQ plays when it starts up, delivers messages, and performs other functions. Because changing sounds takes multiple mouse clicks in different dialog boxes, the best place to find this information is `http://www.icq.com/sounds/use-schemes.html`. This Web address supplies illustrated step-by-step instructions for reconfiguring or disabling your ICQ sounds. Before you change your sounds you might also want to visit `http://www.icq.com/sounds`, a Web address that provides links to downloadable sound schemes (groups of sounds) that you can use for ICQ. (Because certain versions of Netscape can have problems with downloading ICQ sounds, Microsoft Internet Explorer is recommended.) If you'd like to explore the dozens of other changeable settings that ICQ provides, click the **ICQ** button in the program's lower left-hand corner. The displayed menu contains many choices for changing the way ICQ operates, including the Preferences and the Security & Privacy commands.

There is so much to ICQ that it could fill a book (in fact there is a printed user's guide one can order from the software's Web site), but the nice thing about ICQ is that one can use its basic features without having to master all its intricacies. With a little use and some exploration of the software's Web site it will quickly become apparent why ICQ is one of the more popular instant messengers.

Yahoo! Messenger

`http://messenger.yahoo.com`

The fine folks at Yahoo! realized that if they could integrate their instant messaging software with all the other features offered on their Web site, they would have a winning application that appealed to those who want instant access to people as well as information that changes from minute to minute. And that's exactly what Yahoo! Messenger provides (see Figure 11.3).

The Yahoo! Messenger Friends list (bold and smiley face indicate that the person is currently online)

Status menu lets others know when you're online

Window tabs change the Messenger window to display stocks, news, sports, and other information

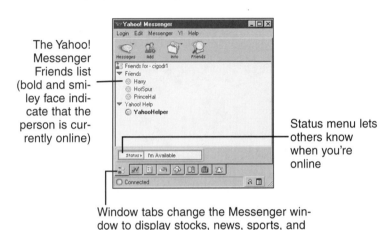

Figure 11.3

Yahoo! Messenger provides a program that's extremely easy to use.

Providing all the usual instant messaging capabilities and an ease of use that is unparalleled, Yahoo! Messenger has a few extra nice features for those who want to socialize online. With no distinction made between online chatting and instant messaging, you can begin a chat session with someone in the same window that contains an instant message you received. A Conference feature allows you to set up an instant message discussion between multiple people who are online (sort of a conference call or instant private chat room) and, in what might be a precedent for things to come, Yahoo! Messenger allows people to actually speak to each other over the Internet. Providing each party has speakers and a microphone, you can select a Yahoo! Messenger Chat Friend (someone on your contact list) and concurrently send text messages while actually talking, as if on a telephone, via its Voice Chat feature.

Yahoo! Messenger also features "alerts": automatic monitors that track other activities you might be taking part in on Yahoo!. Perhaps you've placed a Yahoo! Personal ad. Yahoo! Messenger will notify you when you get a response. Have a Yahoo! mail account? No need to check it while Yahoo! Messenger is on the job, for it'll let you know when mail has arrived. If you follow the financial markets via Yahoo! Finance (also a free service), Yahoo! Messenger will bring you stock quotes (on a 20 minute

151

delay from the current market price). In fact, it will even alert you if a stock of yours reaches an upper or lower limit you've specified or the price change for the day exceeds a pre-set percentage you've defined. And, like all instant messengers, it will even tell you when friends of yours are online.

Other features include news headlines (with links to full stories accessed via your browser), sports scores, and local weather reports delivered directly to Yahoo! Messenger's window. And if you hit it off with someone you've met in Yahoo! Chat (discussed in Chapter 10, "Why is Everyone Talking About Medieval Cookware?"), you can add that person to your Yahoo! Messenger Friends List right from the chat room, making Yahoo! Messenger the perfect program to continue those relationships in days to come.

AOL Instant Messenger

`http://www.aol.com/aim/home.html`

`http://www.aol.com/community/chat/allchats.html`

AOL Instant Messenger (AIM) is to Yahoo! Messenger and ICQ as chicken noodle soup is to vegetable stew: There aren't a lot of ingredients, but what it does have is very tasty. Exceptionally easy to use, AIM's screen has two different views: Online and List Setup (see Figure 11.4). Online lists your buddies (AOL's term for the people you've put on your list to exchange instant messages/chat with) while showing whether or not they are on the Internet. List Setup allows you to add or subtract people to your list, as well as other administrative functions.

One of the important aspects of AIM is the fact that it allows people who don't have America Online to send instant messages and chat with people who do. In addition, AOL has established an extensive site of Web-based chat rooms that can only be accessed if one has the AOL Instant Messenger software. That is why two Web site addresses appear above: The first is to download the program and the second is to access the AOL Instant Messenger's chat rooms once AIM is installed and registered.

AIM, like ICQ, allows users to send and receive files (perfect for those who want to exchange photographs) and, like most of its competitors, has a handy Web search utility that helps you find Web sites, people, and businesses. After each search is completed, AIM displays the results in your Web browser.

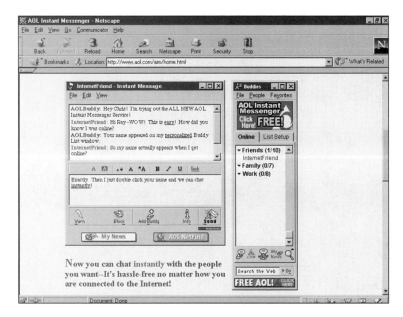

Figure 11.4

AOL Instant Messenger (on the right) allows users to chat over the Internet via a separate chat window (on the left).

MSN Messenger Service

`http://messenger.msn.com`

Having come late to the dance, Microsoft's MSN Messenger Service (see Figure 11.5) debuted in late July 1999, years behind IM stalwarts such as ICQ and AOL Instant Messenger. Prior to using the software, you must first establish a Hotmail (Microsoft's Web-based email) account. Instant messages can be sent only while the recipient is online (many other IM packages will send the message regardless and have it waiting for the recipient when he or she logs on to the Internet), but MSN Messenger uses its direct link to Hotmail to allow users to email a person on it's contact list when that user is offline. Fortunately, MSN Messenger monitors your Hotmail account and notifies you whenever you have mail. Though there are relatively few other features (the obligatory Web search utility and privacy controls, chief among them), it will be interesting to see how Microsoft develops MSN Messenger Service in the months and years to come. After all, this is the same company that created a Web browser years after Netscape and ended up after many revisions with a competitive and useful product.

Figure 11.5

MSN Messenger Service is the new kid on the block for IM programs.

PowWow

`http://www.tribal.com/powwow`

At five years-old and counting, PowWow is one of the elder statesmen of instant messengers (see Figure 11.6). Like ICQ, it has more features than a simple Idiot's Guide write-up can do justice. But unlike ICQ, there is no Simple Mode to guide new users through the labyrinth-like functions that populate this complex program disguised as a simple instant messenger. As such, I recommend you only use PowWow if you are an experienced online chatter/software user or you enjoy figuring things out. PowWow is not for the beginner looking to start messaging and chatting with people five minutes after setup.

Figure 11.6

On the left is one of the menus in PowWow that is accessed via the right mouse button. The window on the right is the actual PowWow program.

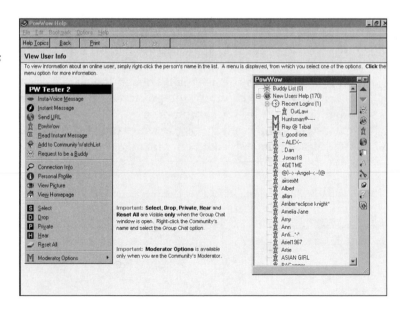

Using a deceivingly uncluttered screen that's free of menu commands and featuring only a simple toolbar stationed vertically on the right side of its window, PowWow requires users to bring up commands by clicking their right mouse button on people they want to chat or instant message with. In addition, the majority of the toolbar's icons contain multiple menu commands. As such, the program can cause the new user to hunt around for commonly used commands, but affords the PowWow guru the opportunity to streamline his or her work process.

In addition to all the standard IM functions, which PowWow has in spades, there are some interesting features and qualities that are unique. One particularly thoughtful touch is what PowWow calls the Answering Machine, a feature that will automatically respond with a message you've composed if someone sends you a correspondence while you're offline or away from your computer and still logged onto the Internet. In this way you can relay useful information (like when you'll be returning to chat/instant message in person) while you're away from the program.

Puppy Love

I am a 32 year-old man and I had never been in love. And though I have experienced friendship, affection, and lust for women, I felt I never had this mysterious bond that is idolized in literature and talked about with such great passion.

I was surfing the net, hoping to find a good deal on a new car, when I received a instant message from a total stranger. "I know who you are and I am loyal" was all it said. Dumbfounded, I stared at the screen wondering what to write back. Before I could think of anything, a second message from the same person appeared. It read, "We belong together." I honestly didn't know if I should be intrigued or terrified. As I began to type a response the third message popped up. "Let's live together. Adopt a puppy!" Evidently I had mentioned in my online profile that I was a dog lover, as well as single, and my new friend thought she'd take advantage of both facts to check me out.

We started chatting and it turned out the puppy adoption offer was sincere, as was everything else about Lisa. After getting to know each other online, we soon made a date to meet in the real world. Needless to say, we are together just over a year and I, for the first time in my life, know what it is to be in love. She never did give away that puppy, as we now share joint custody of this bundle of boundless energy, which we sometimes affectionately refer to as IM.

—*Stan*

Another PowWow feature is cool: Whenever you begin a chat with someone (PowWow offers chat rooms it calls Communities that can be accessed from its Web site and require the software to be running), the program can add your email address to the other chatter's address book and their address to yours. This is great if you want to maintain a relationship with a new person you've met, but not so good if the person turns out to be undesirable. I found this an interesting contrast to the fact that PowWow will not allow another person to add you to their Buddy List for instant messaging unless you first approve it.

PowWow also offers a host of other features including voice chat, text-to-speech (where the computer voices dialogue from group or solo chats via your computer's speakers), and file transmission. Fortunately, an excellent help system in the program assists you in learning these features. I also heartily recommend taking PowWow's Guided Tour, (an online tutorial available from the Web site) to familiarize yourself with the program's basic functions.

Other Instant Messengers

Should you feel you require additional instant messaging choices, have no fear. Instant Messengers, like snowflakes, seem to come in an unending variety. Although they offer basically the same functionality of the previously discussed IMs, each of the following instant messengers has it's own method of facilitating online communication.

Ding!

`http://www.activerse.com`

Another downloadable instant messaging package, Ding! provides traditional IM features, as well as, additional abilities such as sending Web page links via instant messages and exchanging files.

ichat Pager

`http://www.ichat.com/plugin/info/index.html`

ichat Pager, available for download from ichat's Web site, provides many of the standard instant messaging amenities, as well as the ability to send a single message to multiple recipients for the purpose of initiating a private group chat session.

PeopleLink

`http://plnk.peoplelink.com/plnk/peoplelink`

PeopleLink offers Web-based instant messaging that allows you to track, via its Web site, who is online and chat with that person by clicking a link. The site additionally provides a downloadable IM software package so its users can send messages without being on the Web.

The Least You Need to Know

➤ Most commonly used to track when people you know have come online, instant messengers allow you to send a person a correspondence that appears onscreen (usually within seconds of sending it) without the recipient having to retrieve it.

➤ Instant messengers offer levels of privacy not available via standard online chat. Someone using an instant messenger can converse with only the people he or she wants or with the general online community. A user of instant messengers can even become invisible to those who would normally be notified to his or her online presence.

➤ In recent years, instant messengers have evolved into programs that facilitate online text chats, notify users of email activity, exchange files, communicate vocally via microphone and speakers, as well as many other functions.

Chapter 12

All the News That's Fit to Post

In This Chapter

➤ Learn about Internet newsgroups and message boards that allow you to have discussions with others

➤ Explore the possibility of starting your own message board

➤ Discover Web communities with message boards devoted to the concerns of women

---

Message Boards and Newsgroups

There is an old saying that states "There are two types of people in this world: Those who feel no one listens to them and those who feel no one lets them talk." Message boards and newsgroups would serve both groups nicely. A variation on public cork-boards like those found in supermarkets and health clubs, these Internet staples allow you to type up your opinions (called postings) on a range of topics for the world to see. Then anyone who wants to respond can continue the discussion publicly, or, if you've also listed your email address, write to you privately.

When frequenting message boards and newsgroups, you might come across a few new terms within the postings you read:

Thread	A group of messages that refer to a single topic.
Spam	A message that is trying to sell you something and almost always has nothing to do with the discussion at hand. These solicitations can often be for X-rated material or get-rich-quick schemes.
Flame	A vitriolic response to another's posting, usually as a result of spam, an off-topic posting, someone's rude or insensitive commentary, or because the flamer has had a really bad day.

In addition, you might see some of the terms you learned in the previous chapters on chat rooms and instant messaging because many people from those social areas also contribute to the boards and newsgroups.

Usenet and the Web

As discussed in Chapter 2, "My Modem Blinks at Me and I Get Excited," the only difference between message boards and newsgroups is where the information you're reading or posting to is located. Message boards are housed on the World Wide Web whereas newsgroups are stored on another part of the Internet called Usenet.

Usenet, created in 1979, is the original Internet-based bulletin board system. Containing tens of thousands of newsgroups, with more being created all the time, Usenet provides a vehicle for millions of discussions worldwide each week. Until recently, you couldn't access these newsgroups from a Web browser; instead, you needed separate software called a newsgroup reader for this task. (Fortunately, most Web browsers, including Microsoft Internet Explorer and Netscape Communicator, come with a newsgroup reader.) However, for those who want a simpler way to read and compose Usenet newsgroup postings, two Web sites that access this information via your Web browser now exist. They are Talkway and Deja.com.

Talkway

`http://www.talkway.com`

Talkway is one of those sites that is truly fulfilling the promise of the Internet by making millions of people and the information they create easily accessible (see Figure 12.1). With more than 35,000 newsgroups at its disposal, Talkway has structured its site to make finding the discussion you want extremely easy. Newsgroups, which often sport hard-to-decipher Usenet names, are given Talkway monikers for easy subject identification. Also, a search engine lets you find whatever discussion topic you want and general interest links let you wander through the vast listings of newsgroups in case you just want to see what you can discover by accident.

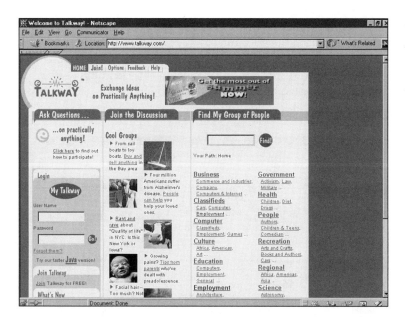

Figure 12.1

At Talkway, you can participate in discussions taking place in more than 35,000 newsgroups.

You can browse the different postings and discussions but to contribute your own viewpoints, you have to become a Talkway site member, which is absolutely free and well worth the time. In addition to being able to create your own discussion entries, membership allows you to maintain a list of your favorite newsgroups (allowing you to return to them with a single click), keep track of what messages you've read, and receive the Talkway email digest SneakPeak. SneakPeak summarizes the most active threads among the discussions in your list of favorite newsgroups.

One particularly nice feature of Talkway is reply notification. Most message boards and newsgroups require you to return to your original posting sporadically to see if anyone has written a response. If you choose, Talkway will automatically send you an email notifying you when anyone has responded to your message.

Because Usenet is filled with colorful, or what some might call obscene, language, filtering options allow you to stop some, but never all, offensive expression. And for those with Java-enabled browsers (see Chapter 10, "Why Is Everyone Talking About Medieval Cookware?"), Talkway has a speedy Java version of their site as well. All things considered, Talkway makes Usenet newsgroups fun and easy to use.

Deja.com

`http://www.deja.com`

Deja.com gets its name from the fact that several incarnations prior to its current Web site, it started out as a newsgroup search engine (see Figure 12.2). The idea was that if you wanted to look up information on a topic, you could perform a search and a listing of previous postings on the subject (dating back years, if necessary) from different newsgroups would be created. In this way, you would be saved the trouble of continually posting questions to and visiting multiple newsgroups in the hopes of finding information that already existed as an earlier posting. Deja.com still has this wonderful ability, but it has evolved into much more.

Figure 12.2

Deja.com lets you participate in new discussions or read through those from days past.

Newsgroups and Junk Email

You might want to think twice about posting your everyday email address to a newsgroup or message board. Individuals and companies can employ programs that are designed to scan through newsgroups and message boards to collect email addresses for the purpose of sending out junk email. After your email address is obtained this way, it can in turn be sold to other companies, resulting in dozens of junk emails sent to your account each day. Because many people enjoy getting email directly from those who've read their postings (and many newsgroup and message board sites require a valid email address to use their services), it is often a wise precaution to obtain a second Web-based email address for newsgroup and message board use.

The key to getting the most out of the site is, once again, filling out a registration form and joining what Deja.com refers to as "My Deja." Upon becoming a member, you can subscribe to a newsgroup (bookmarking its location for quickly returning there later) and use search functions that let you look for entire newsgroups or particular postings by author or date.

Deja.com's features do not stop at Usenet. Using the terms "Forums" and "Discussions" interchangeably to refer to newsgroups, Deja.com has added a distinction called "Communities" to describe message boards that are not a part of Usenet, but are hosted on the Web by the site. These communities are created by Deja.com's members and raise the total of newsgroups and message boards available on the site to 80,000. Although other sites feature this function (see Yahoo! Clubs and Delphi later in this chapter), Deja.com is the only one to combine this with accessibility to Usenet.

Other features include the ability to post and respond to newsgroup messages from your email program, and like Talkway, it has a feature to notify you by email when someone has added to a discussion thread you're following. Deja.com will even supply you with an email account if you do not want your postings to reveal your everyday email address.

Although Deja.com is a tremendous resource for talking to anyone who uses newsgroups, it could be a frustrating site for the Web beginner. Navigation within the site is inconsistent from page to page, causing some confusion. (For instance, the "My Deja" link on the site's opening screen is in the upper-right corner of the page, but elsewhere it's in the lower-left corner, often requiring a hefty scroll to find it.) In addition, the site operates slowly at times, making the user wait much longer than comparable sites for a page to load. These limitations aside, for those who want an excellent research tool, as well as one for meeting like-minded souls, Deja.com delivers the goods.

It Takes a Community

As you might know, many of the free services discussed in this book are made possible by Web-based advertising dollars. Whether you're in a chat room, instant messenger window, or just perusing a personal ad, it's not uncommon to see an advertisement that was sold to underwrite your socializing. Because companies are trying to get as many people as possible to their Web sites in the hope of charging more for their ads, they have developed the idea of Web-based communities (sometimes called portals). Essentially a model of symbiosis, Web-based communities try to provide you with everything you need (email, chat, personals, services, message boards, and so on) in the hope that you'll return day after day to the site. In this way, Web communities have a greater volume of people seeing their ads, and you have more people to socialize with. These communities are often based around general interest topics but also can revolve around gender, geography, and special interest. As such, they make a great place to start exploring the world of message boards.

Yahoo! GeoCities, Yahoo! Clubs, and Yahoo! Message Boards

`http://www.geocities.com/neighborhoods`

`http://clubs.yahoo.com`

`http://messages.yahoo.com`

With its acquisition of GeoCities (now rechristened Yahoo! GeoCities), a site known for its message boards and strong community spirit, Yahoo! hosts one of the best places for posted Web discussion (see Figure 12.3). Each of its 41 neighborhoods, with topics ranging from computers to sports to fashion, has its own message board. Like all the community sites in this section, you must join the site to post responses or start discussions, but as usual, this is a free and painless process. If you've already joined Yahoo! for any of its other offerings, your ID will allow you to participate here as well.

Figure 12.3

This sample club, from Yahoo! Club's tutorial, shows many of the site features that are available, including club message boards.

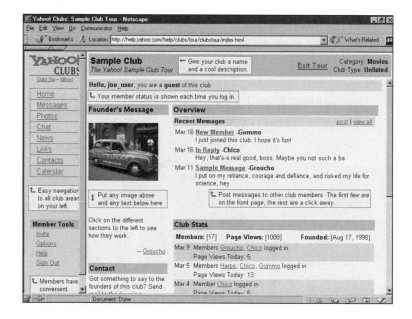

Well Posted, Well Read

I live in a small town surrounded by those some might call good-old boys. People here are helpful, kind, and full of life. But I like to read books as opposed to watching television or riding 20 miles into the city to see what's playing at the movie house. And there aren't any people here who share my literary passions. Thank God for the Internet! I belong to several newsgroups where we discuss everything from Grisham to Dickens. Over the years I've come to think of these people as my friends. Going far beyond literary discussion, we share each other's lives, giving presents during holidays and offering consolation in times of grief. I even have pictures of most of our group hanging on my refrigerator! And though I'll probably never meet many of them, these people have given me a connection to something that really is hard to find where I now live. They share my values.

—*Polly*

The proverbial tree fort of the Internet, Yahoo! Clubs was created for those who want to access information on very specific topics. You can join one of the hundreds of clubs that already exist (there's a good search engine to help you find one you'll like) or you can form your own. For instance, if you have a fascination with insects and you want to have a place where other insect aficionados share their knowledge and trade amusing multi-legged anecdotes, you could create an insect club (although you'd be too late—at least two already exist). Besides access to the club message board, membership lets you post pictures and participate in private club chat. And if you are the club founder, you also can send announcements via email to all the club's members and restrict membership to as many or as few as you like.

Yahoo! Message Boards fill in all the gaps not covered by Yahoo! GeoCities and Yahoo! Clubs. Containing thousands of boards, almost every general interest and many specific topics are covered. And therein lies the problem. Although many of the boards in this section of Yahoo! are burgeoning with discussion (for instance, as of this writing they have more than 7,000 popular message boards devoted to different financial sectors and stocks), a good number remain totally empty. As such, you might be better off finding discussion on lesser known topics at Yahoo! Clubs, even though there might be a counterpart message board already listed with Yahoo! Message Boards.

Delphi Forums

`http://www.delphi.com`

`http://www.delphi.com/dir-app/search`

Strictly speaking, Delphi Forums is not a Web community. However, this site, with more than two million users and 80,000 message boards (which it calls forums), provides the message board services for many other Web communities (see Figure 12.4). About.com, Xoom.com, Fox News, and others all access Delphi Forums when a member of one of those communities uses a message board. The beauty of becoming a free member of Delphi Forums is that you access its discussions, as well as those from all the community sites that contribute to it.

Figure 12.4

Delphi Forums provides the message board backbone for many major Web sites.

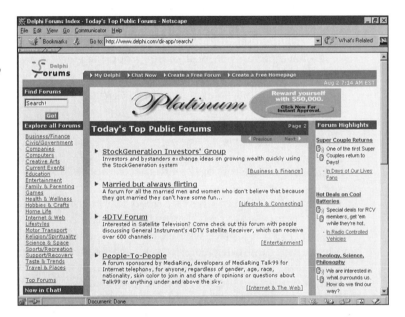

The two Web addresses listed for Delphi Forums offer access to message boards, but the second one features a more detailed index of choices. Both pages offer a search engine for finding the message board of your choice. And like Yahoo! Clubs and Deja.com, you can create your own forum for whatever discussion topic you choose. Delphi Forums also offers chat rooms for those who want a one-stop destination for discussion.

Women.com, iVillage, and Oxygen

`http://www.women.com/membership/boards.html`

`http://www.ivillage.com/boards`

`http://www.oxygen.com/chat/index.html`

In the last few years, the Web has awoken to the fact that women want a place of their own to voice their opinions. Three of the most popular women's sites—Women.com, iVillage, and Oxygen—have attracted a large number of members in great part due to the help of their message boards (see Figure 12.5). Featuring message boards with titles like Technodivas, The Self-Employed Woman, and Battle of the Bulge (all from iVillage), these sites cater not only to the gender-based concerns of women, but also to any other topic they might find interesting. This means you'll find message boards at these sites dealing with general interest topics as well—except the viewpoints expressed will almost always be exclusively from women.

Figure 12.5

These are some of the topics women are talking about on the Women.com message boards.

Women.com's message boards are extremely straightforward, presenting the reader with a date-stamped index detailing the subject of each message and who wrote it. This allows you to quickly determine if you want to read a message or skip it. Because postings are arranged in date order with the most recent messages listed at the top of the screen, reviewing postings is as easy as a simple scroll.

If only iVillage had followed Women.com's technical example. Although the site offers a broader and, to my taste, a more interesting range of message board topics, the technical setup is a little backwards. Older postings are listed at the top of the screen, making readers scroll to the bottom of a page and work backwards through links to read the most recent postings first. The same is true for creating a discussion message—the button to create a posting is available only at the bottom of the Web page, as well.

Oxygen, only a few months old as of this writing, is currently serving as a portal to the message boards for four other women-oriented sites: Thrive Online, Oprah, ka-Ching, and Moms Online. By taking this segmented approach, Oxygen looks to attract women who want to discuss, respectively, their body and wellness, issues discussed on Oprah Winfrey's show, financial issues, and topics of concern for women who have or are about to have children. Although both Women.com and iVillage have message boards dealing with these subjects, Oxygen is placing its emphasis there while leaving the other general interest topics to its competitors.

Other Community Sites

The following community sites all feature additional opportunities for message board discussion.

Go Network Message Boards

http://www.go.com/Community/Message

Excite Message Boards

http://boards.excite.com/boards

Nettaxi Online Communities

http://messageboards.nerdworld.com/nettaxi/

The Uncounted Thousands

Despite the newsgroup and message board sites previously listed, Web-based discussion groups have become so prevalent that there are uncounted thousands more that haven't been mentioned. Got a favorite sports team? It probably has a site with a message board. Enjoy a musician, movie, or television show? Ditto. How about politics, religion, and finance, just to name three more? You already know the answer. To find a message board for a topic not covered by the sites in this book (although they are a good first place to look), just use the search engine of your choice to seek one out. In case you've never used a search engine, here are a few suggestions:

Yahoo!

http://www.yahoo.com

Excite

http://www.excite.com

Go Network

`http://www.go.com`

Google!

`http://www.google.com`

Usenet References: Usenet Without a Web

`http://www.faqs.org/usenet`

Those new to the Web might not be aware that there is an entire subculture that has risen out of Usenet since its inception more than two decades ago (see Figure 12.6). With the advent of the Web, many of the software packages, procedures, and traditions of this community have no interest to the new Internet user. However, for those who might want to learn more about Usenet, its manual workings and other software used to access it, the address at `http://www.faqs.org/usenet` is a good place to start. For those who would like to explore using the newsreader that comes with Netscape Communicator or Microsoft Outlook and Outlook Express (which serves as the newsgroup reader for Internet Explorer), just hit your **F1** key in either of those programs and search the help files supplied for the information you seek.

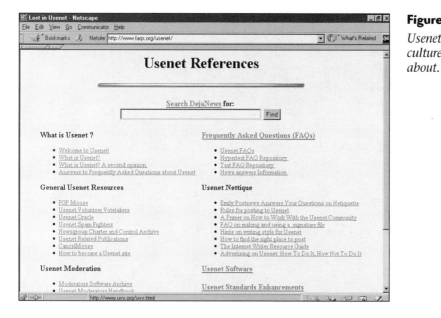

Figure 12.6

Usenet has a whole subculture one can learn about.

The Least You Need to Know

➤ Message boards are discussion groups housed on the Web while newsgroups are housed on another part of the Internet called Usenet.

➤ Although both message boards and newsgroups can be accessed from Web browsers these days, newsgroups, around since 1979, also can be used with newsreader software.

➤ Web communities that provide multiple services ranging from message boards to email have sprung up in an effort to keep Web surfers coming back to the same site day after day.

Chapter 13

"Funny, I Never Expected to Meet Someone Here."

In This Chapter

➤ New technologies for meeting people with your browser

➤ An online place to plan get-togethers online

➤ Sites where people can share common interests

Some Enchanted Evening

A young woman purchasing a package of gum at the local stationery store drops her purse and upon looking into the eyes of the helpful stranger who retrieves it for her, falls madly in love. Or a regular guy with nothing to do on a Saturday afternoon decides to read his newspaper in the park when a woman interrupts him to inquire if the seat next to him is taken and before long they're making dinner plans. Romantic serendipity: we've all heard about it or experienced it firsthand. But on the Internet, it's almost impossible to just run into a stranger by accident. Most people believe their choices are restricted to either seeking out companionship via an obvious resource like a chat room or surfing in isolation.

But the World Wide Web provides a third choice. Dozens of sites devoted to special-ized interests or new uses of the Internet's technology have appeared, drawing legions of like-minded souls together. So even though meeting people this way is not exactly coincidental, there's no reason not to help fate out a bit.

Teaching an Old Browser New Tricks

There was a time, not too long ago, when all a graphical browser like Netscape or Internet Explorer could do was display text and simple graphics. Now browsers play sounds, show movies and animated graphics, and allow all manner of interactivity from simple Web-based quizzes to full-fledged chat environments. But recently, two programs have emerged that let you interact with other Web surfers in totally new ways. They are called Gooey and Odigo.

Gooey

`http://www.hypernix.com`

Surfing the Web is often like traveling alone: You discover a really cool site and there's no one to share your excitement with. The makers of Gooey are trying to change all that. A chat environment that follows the user from site to site, Gooey lets users talk to each other while exploring different parts of the Web (see Figure 13.1). Just as in a regular chat room, Gooey supplies a chat window that displays ongoing conversations and a list displaying the names of chatters. But as soon as you go to a new Web site, Gooey displays any Gooey users now looking at that particular part of the Web. In this way, whoever is in your list of chat participants at any particular moment is looking at the very same Web site you are.

Figure 13.1

This screen capture shows people browsing and using Gooey to chat while at the Gooey Web site. The bottom window contains the dialogue and the list of chat participants (with a title bar that reads "Nicks") floats at the right of the screen. Gooey also can be configured to have chatters and dialogue in a single window.

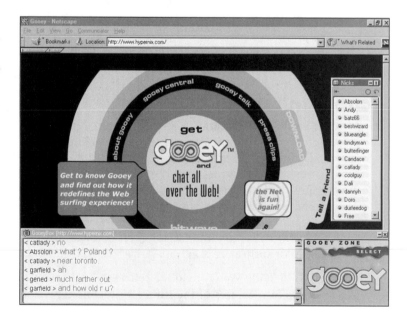

Unlike most Web-based text chat environments, Gooey requires the user to download software, but the program is free and installation is easy. In addition to talking to friends old and new while exploring the Web, Gooey provides many of the standard chatting amenities including private chat and the ability to block people from talking to you. For those who want to seek out other Gooey chatters, a feature called Hitwave will bring up a window listing the top 20 sites currently being discussed by Gooey visitors. Click the link and your browser takes you right to the site and the conversation surrounding it.

Last, Gooey's chat window has a section called the Gooey Zone, which offers cartoons, games, and other entertainment one can enjoy while surfing. "The Web is the people who surf it" states the slogan for Hypernix, the company that created Gooey. And Gooey allows you to meet those people as you discover Web sites together.

The Next Gooey or Odigo?

Where will future innovative online socializing opportunities come from? Although it's impossible to say, there are two Web addresses that regularly list new and interesting Web sites: `http://dir.yahoo.com/new` and `http://home.netscape.com/netcenter/new.html`. If you're looking for new places to meet people online, these two sites, from Yahoo! and Netscape respectively, are often the first to publicize them. And although they might have no new social opportunities on any given day, these pages will always list fun new Web sites to visit.

Odigo

`http://www.odigo.com`

What do you get when you cross an instant messenger with a browser? If you said a speedy shopper, then you've not heard of Odigo (see Figure 13.2). So if you're still reading past the previous example of second grade humor, let me tell you about a program that like Gooey, lets you meet people while surfing the Web, but takes a more one-on-one approach to the task.

Figure 13.2

On the left are some of the cartoon portraits you can use to represent yourself within Odigo. On the right is the Odigo program, with its radar scope at the bottom.

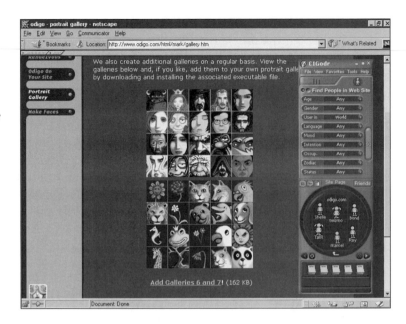

Odigo, which means a "guide" in Greek, tracks people browsing the same Web site you are. After downloading and installing Odigo's software, you fill out a personal profile detailing whatever information you'd like to divulge including gender, age (or age range), profession, hobbies, zodiac sign, and dating availability. You also can select a cartoon portrait (much like the chat avatars mentioned in Chapter 10, "Why Is Everyone Talking About Medieval Cookware?") that will represent you to others using Odigo. After this is done, not only can you bump into other Odigo users as you explore Web sites, but you can search for new people to meet online based on the profile criteria they have filled out.

After you've found someone you want to communicate with, you can request a chat session, send an instant message, transmit a file, or pass along a Web address. You can let people know in advance of contacting you what your mood is (choices range from indifferent to fabulous to angry), what kind of chat you're looking for (romance, small talk, and so on), or you can hide your presence altogether making other surfers unaware that you're online. Odigo has no group chat capability, which actually makes sense considering the combination of its search facilities and user-tracking features focuses the program on allowing you to connect with one person at a time. As such it makes a great complement to Gooey, which doesn't track individual users, but instead tracks group discussions.

Odigo does have a bit of a learning curve and could be confusing to users not willing to take the time to explore its controls and features (many of which can only be operated by clicking very small icons). Chief among these is an innovative radar-like screen that tracks online users, representing them as pulsating dots that turn into generic cartoon boys and girls when clicked. However, for those who invest the time,

Odigo is a great way to meet people online and can make surfing the Web a shared experience.

Play a Game

To quote Star Trek's Mr. Spock, the more complex the mind, the greater the need for the simplicity of play. But why not meet some people online while you're attending to the needs of your complex mind? The following sites allow you to do just that.

The Mystery Match Game

`http://www.intermingle.com`

Take a good helping of The Dating Game, add a pinch of Mystery Date, flavor with email, and you've got the recipe for The Mystery Match Game, an online competition where three contestants vie for the opportunity to converse via email with an unknown romantic prospect (see Figure 13.3).

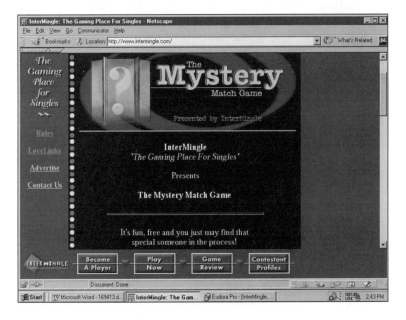

Figure 13.3

Who lies behind the door to The Mystery Match Game? Perhaps your next date.

After you are registered at the free site, you can choose to initiate a game by selecting three contestants from profiles detailing specifics of gender, age, general location, and personal interests. Your contestants will then be notified by email that an unknown Mystery Date has chosen them to compete in a Mystery Match Game. Each contestant must answer three questions you've chosen from a list of 50. Queries range from the straightforward ("Who is your role model and why?") to the suggestive ("I've been very bad. What would you do to teach me a lesson?"). Contestants have 72 hours to answer your questions and all members of the site can see how the game is progressing online via their browser. After you select a winner, he or she is emailed your handle (so that your profile might be browsed) and email address. Although your real identity is never revealed (and the losing contestants do not get any contact information), you then have the opportunity to converse via email with the winning contestant to see if you want to take things farther. Or if you prefer, you can fill out a profile and hope that someone will choose you as a contestant. Either way, The Mystery Match Game provides a fun way to meet people.

Traditional Gaming

In addition to the other pastimes mentioned in this chapter, many sites provide traditional games such as Chess, Checkers, Bridge, and Backgammon that you can play online with human opponents. Two of the best sites are the MSN Gaming Zone (`http://www.zone.com`) and Yahoo! Games (`http://games.yahoo.com`). Both sites offer a good selection of free games, and allow chatting between opponents. It should be noted that MSN Gaming Zone requires you to be running a computer with Microsoft Windows installed. Yahoo!'s games work with all computers.

The Dating Game Online and The Station

`http://www.station.sony.com/datinggame`

Ah, the 60s. Free love. Psychedelica. The Dating Game! And now you can virtually enjoy all three more than 30 years after the original television show's inception with The Dating Game Online (see Figure 13.4). Unlike the Mystery Match Game, which is geared towards finding you an actual date, The Dating Game Online is more about socializing and having a good time. However, Sony Online Entertainment, which hosts the site, felt there was a good enough possibility of people making a groove thang that prior to participating, all contestants are required to click an agreement saying the site is not responsible for anything that happens as a result of participants engaging in on or offline hijinks.

Figure 13.4

Contestants asking and answering questions in The Dating Game Online.

After you are registered at the site, go immediately to editing your profile, which will specify your gender and allow you to create a cartoon that will stand in for you during the game. Even if you meet no one, this process is worth the visit as you can construct your avatar in a Mr. Potato Head fashion that lets you select your hair, mouth, eyes, and body. This also gives the game an added dimension as contestants have created their likenesses to look as they want others to see them.

Much like graphical chat, The Dating Game Online places you in a window with three other contestants, all of whose dialogue appears above the head of their cartoon representation. As in the television show, one player puts questions to the other three and based on their answers, selects one to go on a virtual date, which takes place in a chat room. Prior to the virtual date, the lucky couple takes a compatibility test, answering 10 either-or questions to find out if they think alike. The more they answer the same, the better the cartoon backdrop for their virtual date. Once on the date, they can chat privately about whatever they want, without others listening in. Winning couples can even email themselves a screen capture commemorating the virtual date.

As discussed in Chapter 10, you'll need a Java-compatible browser to enjoy The Dating Game Online. And because the action happens in real-time, you might have to wait for other players to show up. But don't lose your cool. And don't let The Man dictate what sites you'll visit. Check out The Dating Game Online. Peace, baby.

The Station@Sony.com

`http://www.station.sony.com`

The parent site of the previously mentioned Dating Game Online, The Station@Sony.com offers many multi-player games, including Jeopardy Online and Wheel of Fortune Online, that allow players to socialize over the Internet via graphical chat while competing. A great site for gaming and general socializing.

em@il games

`http://email.games.com`

Hasbro Interactive has come up with a series of classic board games that you can play via email. Though most of the games must be purchased, including Scrabble, Battleship, Chess, Checkers, and Backgammon, Up Words, a vertical crossword game, is free. And though you can't yet meet people this way (though if Hasbro is smart, they'll start message boards where players can contact each other to find games), this is a good way to socialize with those you already know, exchanging email notes with each turn of a game played. Every email reveals, via a small attachment, the full progress of the game, including a graphical representation of the playing board and all moves taken so far. So even if days pass between moves, game play, as well as banter, remains easy.

Plan a Get-Together with Evite.com

`http://www.evite.com`

Geared towards encouraging socializing online or off, Evite.com allows you to use email and the Web to plan events. Got a group who'd like to talk online at the same time? Planning a party in the offline world? How about that vacation with friends from across the country? All of these and more are possible with Evite.com (see Figure 13.5).

Using a simple Web page form, users of the free service fill out the specifics of the event including location, date, and time, and a list of invitees' email addresses. If you want to invite someone who doesn't have email, Evite.com will also fax the invitation at no charge. After all the information, which also can include a personal note; directions to the event; and even a map, are input, the invitations are sent at the click of a button. RSVPs are taken when the invitees log on to the site for your event and accept, decline, or state they are undecided. Other features include tracking event details such as what food participants should bring; allowing other guests to see the list of invitees; or permitting others to add to your guest list by using Evite.com to invite additional participants.

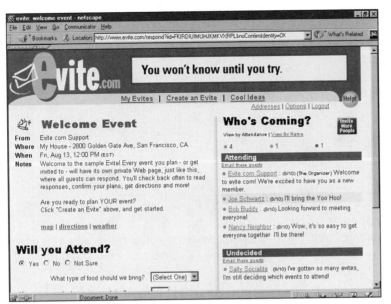

Figure 13.5

An Evite.com Web page lets people who RSVP know who is already attending an event.

Talk Up a Collection at eBay

`http://pages.ebay.com/community/chat/index.html`

Online auction site eBay has become one of the most popular Web addresses for buying and selling collectibles on the Internet—not only for the specialized sales venue it supplies, but also for its message boards (which eBay confusingly refers to on some pages as chat). Those interested in antiques, books, dolls, stamps, jewelry, and all manner of collectible items have discussion boards devoted to each topic. In addition, the site offers The eBay Café, a message board devoted to general socializing. Registration is free and one does not have to participate in an auction to join the various discussions.

Catch Up with the News

The Web supplies a great meeting place for both hardcore news junkies and those with an interest in current events. The following sites feature mostly message boards and chat, so if you have an opinion to share on a topical subject, these are some very good places to find like-minded souls and debate opponents.

CNN Interactive Discussion Message Boards

`http://www.cnn.com/boards`

MSNBC

`http://www.msnbc.com/chat`

National Public Radio Online

http://www.npr.org/yourturn

The New York Times

http://forums.nytimes.com/comment

Time.com

http://cgi.pathfinder.com/time/community

Meet a Jock

Few communities have a more passionate base than those comprised of sports fans. Although many of the popular sports chat and message boards are located on the sites discussed in Chapters 10 and 12, many professional clubs in major markets have sites devoted to their teams that foster discussion and debate. In New York, both Major League Baseball teams, The New York Mets (http://www.mets.com) and The New York Yankees (http://www.yankees.com), feature chat rooms and message boards devoted to their respective team (see Figure 13.6). If you're a fan of a professional sports team, search the Web to see if they've established a site. You might be surprised to find others have preceded you there with all manner of commentary. If you're looking to just talk sports in general, check out the previously mentioned chat and message board sites, or the sports-dedicated ones that follow.

Figure 13.6

Many professional sports clubs like The New York Mets (http:// www.mets.com) feature message boards and chat that allow fans to share their passion online.

CNNSI.com

```
http://www.cnnsi.com/your_turn
```

```
http://www.cnnsi.com/your_turn/message_boards
```

Interactive Internet Sports

```
http://www.iis-sports.com
```

MSNBC 24-Hour Sports Chat

```
http://www.msnbc.com/chat/sports.asp
```

Hang Out with the Geeks

If you enjoy computers and technology, there's an overabundance of people sharing those common interests via Usenet newsgroups (Chapter 12). In addition, hundreds of hardware and software companies supply message boards so users, enthused or aggravated by their products, can discuss their opinions as well as technological features and uses. For those who would like a couple of additional sites devoted to these burgeoning topics, look to the sites that follow. The ZDNet chat site is particularly interesting in that it hosts graphical computer and technology chat rooms.

CNET Message Boards

```
http://forums.cnet.com
```

ZDNet

```
http://www.zdnet.com/cc/forums.html
```

```
http://chat.zdnet.com
```

WinMag Discussions

```
http://bbs.winmag.com
```

Local Networking

Online networking has always been a good source of business leads, but never did I think it would impact my private life. I was chatting about stock options when I sarcastically said, "I wish getting a date were as easy as predicting puts and calls." Well, a trader, who I only know from online, says he has a sister near where I live and would I like to meet her. Before I know it, her phone number is emailed to me, we talk on the phone, and we've now been going out for four months. It pays to network!

—*Bob*

Talk About Finance

In good times and bad, people are always talking about stocks and finance. Though there are dozens of places to discuss financial topic matter, the following sites provide particularly well-traveled message boards.

Raging Bull

`http://www.ragingbull.com/community`

Stock-Talk

`http://www.stock-talk.com/stocks/list.shtml`

The Motley Fool

`http://boards.fool.com`

Yahoo! Finance Message Boards

`http://messages.yahoo.com/yahoo/Business_and_Finance/index.html`

The Least You Need to Know

➤ You can now use your Web browser to meet people online who are surfing the same Web site as you.

➤ Using the Internet to plan your own on or offline get-togethers is easy.

➤ Dozens of Web sites geared towards people with special interests provide chat rooms and message boards to bring like-minded souls together.

DING DING

Chapter 14

The First Time I Laid Eyes on Your Font, I Heard Bells.

In This Chapter

➤ Discover great sites to help you plan your wedding

➤ Learn where to find online registries and other wedding services

➤ Explore wedding sites devoted to the groom and best man

For some, the ultimate goal of meeting people online is a trip down the aisle without the aid of a shotgun or hypnosis. For those about to reach that objective (perhaps as a result of this book's first 13 chapters), *The Complete Idiot's Guide* presents some online resources for helping you through the planning and implementation of your nuptials.

The Knot

http://www.theknot.com

There aren't many places you can go and find eight women talking about strippers, but that was the scene one night as I stopped by to check out The Knot's chat rooms devoted to all things wedding-oriented. The heated discussion, revolving around one soon-to-be bride's concern about her fiancée's bachelor party, goes to the heart of The Knot's philosophy: Yes, planning your wedding should be fun, but it's also damn stressful and we'll support you any way we can. As such, The Knot (see Figure 14.1) provides a full array of services to help future brides and grooms. In addition to the aforementioned wedding chat room, The Knot provides message boards featuring dis-cussions on hot button issues like interfaith ceremonies and eloping as well as standard postings on topics including ceremony music, catering, and whether or not to use a registry. The latter is of special interest to The Knot, as one of the features they prominently showcase is their own wedding gift registry featuring more than 10,000 potential gifts. Prospective newlyweds select traditional and non-traditional gifts they'd like to receive and all their Internet-savvy friends can purchase anything on their list (or something entirely different) via the Web or toll-free number. A search engine for wedding guests makes finding the correct registry a snap.

Figure 14.1

The Knot provides a one-stop Web site for planning your wedding.

The Knot, which is free to members, provides a plethora of other services including an 11,000 strong searchable bridal gown database featuring pictures of each gown; wedding vendor and photographer lists; nuptial budget planners and checklists; and articles on every conceivable wedding topic. One of the most interesting features of the site is what The Knot refers to as Personal Wedding Pages. Couples can create a three-page wedding Web site hosted without charge by The Knot. Ceremony information, guest lists, and stories about how the couple-to-be fell in love, as well as any other information, can be posted for all the world to see. Or you can password-protect the information so only invited guests can access your wedding details. This is just one more detail that makes it easy to see why people feel comfortable with The Knot.

With This Web I Thee Wed

It's the same old story. Kim and Todd fall in love. Kim and Todd get married. Kim and Todd build a Web site detailing all they've learned on the road to their nuptials. A visit to their Web site (`http://home1.gte.net/kimred`) provides something you won't find at the other wedding sites in this book: a detailed account by the bride and groom of their wedding as it was planned and successfully carried out. Along with the tips they learned, Todd and Kim also publish the actual budget that was spent on their wedding, which was attended by 150 guests. And if this one account is not enough, visit the Newlywed Web Ring at `http://www.geocities.com/~toddandrobyn/newlywed.html`. On this page you'll find a link to a "List of Newlywed Sites" where others share their personal wedding experiences.

WeddingChannel.com

`http://www.weddingchannel.com`

Whereas The Knot tries to give support both emotionally and logistically, WeddingChannel.com concentrates strictly on the chores of traditional wedding planning (see Figure 14.2). But that focus gives it a depth in that area that is hard to parallel.

Many of the amenities featured by The Knot also can be found at WeddingChannel.com, including creating your own wedding Web pages, articles on wedding-related topics, and a gift registry. But where The Knot's registry features computer components and camping equipment, WeddingChannel.com's is more traditional focusing on products for the home and gifts for the wedding's participants. In fact the entire site seems more geared toward classic weddings with in-depth editorial coverage on topics as varied as selecting a diamond to hosting an afternoon tea for your bridesmaids. There is even an article on how weddings are evolving called "The New Traditions."

One of the best features of WeddingChannel.com, however, is the site's ease of use. Though The Knot has an astounding array of choices, it can be a bit confusing as a single page could feature a couple dozen links. WeddingChannel.com, by contrast, places an easy navigation bar across the top of its Web site providing a guide to the site's prime destinations. Add all this to services that include travel planning for wedding guests and you've got another great wedding planning site.

Figure 14.2

WeddingChannel.com makes navigating through a wedding, and a wedding Web site, easy.

The Ultimate Internet Wedding Guide

`http://www.ultimatewedding.com`

For some it's the caterer. For others it's renting the hall. And for audiophiles the most difficult aspect of wedding planning can be the music. Fear not, gentle reader, as The Ultimate Internet Wedding Guide has taken upon itself the creation of The Ultimate Wedding Song Library, a collection of hundreds of can't miss wedding tunes arranged in categories including the couple's first dance, cake cutting, and songs for tossing the garter (see Figure 14.3). In an ingenious bit of cross marketing, The Ultimate Internet Wedding Guide has linked each song title to Amazon.com, an online retailer of books and music, which has made available sound bytes from each selection so you can preview the songs online. If you decide to buy them on the spot, so much the better.

Of course if you can't decide what to say to your betrothed just before you tie the knot, that could present an even greater problem. Fortunately the site also features a large selection of prose and poetry for wedding vows or ceremonial speeches by others. There is also a wedding humor and jokes section, but these pieces are more likely to amuse you in your solitude than to provide grist for writing the perfect toast.

Another nice feature of The Ultimate Internet Wedding Guide is the section entitled "Wedding Links Galore!" Titanium wedding bands, a service that makes your engagement photo into souvenir magnets for your wedding guests, and hundreds of other products and services you might never think of (as well as all the traditional wedding needs) are represented by Web page links to the companies that supply them. Combine all this with many of the resources featured in the previously mentioned sites and The Ultimate Wedding Guide does a good job of living up to its name.

Figure 14.3

Not sure what music to play as you or your spouse tosses the garter? The Ultimate Internet Wedding Guide has these suggestions and many more.

GARTER

Look for the ♫ symbol to hear sound clips online!

Visit the audio help page to assistance and free software to listen to clips

Please share with us the music you will be using!

Number	TITLE	ARTIST	ALBUM	SOUND CLIPS
1	The Stripper	David Rose	Bachelor Pad Pleasures	♫Available
2	Legs	ZZ Top	Eliminator	-
3	Theme from Mission Impossible	Danny Elfman	Mission Impossible (Soundtrack)	♫Available
4	You Sexy Thing	Hot Chocolate	The Full Monty (Soundtrack)	♫Available
5	You Can Leave Your Hat On	Joe Cocker	The Full Monty (Soundtrack)	♫Available
6	Oh, Pretty Woman	Roy Orbison	The All-Time Greatest Hits	♫Available
7	Hungry Eyes	Eric Carmen	Definitive Collection	-
8	Wild Thing	The Troggs	The Best of the Troggs	♫Available
9	Guys Do It All the Time	Mindy McCready	Ten Thousand Angels	♫Available
10	Heaven	Bryan Adams	Reckless	♫Available
11	Kiss	Prince	Parade	-

The Words She Longed to Hear

I met Jim in the spring. I was chatting online not looking for anything special, only chat buddies with common interests. We talked for almost four hours that first night. He wooed me with email cards and flowers that he sent to my office, but after we exchanged phone numbers I became anxious. I called him well over a 100 times and kept hanging up before it would ring. When I admitted to him online how nervous I was he called me and put me right at ease.

We had our first date: lunch at a sushi bar. It was nice. And though I didn't see him for another two weeks we kept chatting online and talking on the phone. Once we began dating I knew what it was. So did he, but neither of us had the nerve to say so. After the first month together we spent our first night together. It was heaven. I knew the moment he looked into my eyes and I lost myself that I was in love. Nothing else mattered. I broke down a few weeks later and declared my love for him. I was so scared, I was shaking. He smiled at me and said, "I know you do baby." Well, he never said it back and I wondered if he felt the same for me.

continues

continued

Months passed, the relationship grew, but he still had never said he loved me. Could I have been wrong about him? Did he think of me as a casual fling? Had I given my heart too easily? Then it happened. A simple "I love you too." I almost fell dead away. He had finally muttered the words I yearned to hear. I didn't think I had heard it right, so I asked what he said, and he said it again. I began to cry. This was the happiest day of my life. Of course we are planning on getting married, so I'm looking forward to an even happier one.

—Judy

ModernBride.com

http://www.modernbride.com

For years Modern Bride magazine has been advising women on all aspects of their big day. Continuing that mission within their Web site, ModernBride.com presents a nice mix of unique editorial content and links to other sites that offer online wedding resources.

As with the printed magazine, ModernBride.com has a lot to say about wedding fashion. Articles on many aspects of marriage attire including advice on selecting the bride's headpiece, lingerie, and shoes, as well as how the mother of the bride should dress, were in evidence. For those who are new to getting married, tutorials such as the gown glossary (which explains the different parts of a wedding gown) provide basic information for making informed sartorial choices (see Figure 14.4).

Many of the amenities one would expect, including wedding planning advice and message boards containing all manner of wedding-based discussion, populate the site. Unfortunately, some of the site's best content is hidden from easy access. The Romance and Relationships section, which contains the funny Bridezilla cartoon, Lisa & Mike's To-be-Wed Files (diary entries from a couple who are planning their wedding), and such features as a bridesmaid quiz (to test if you've selected the right person for the job), can be found only if you dig well into ModernBride.com. But for those who explore the site (especially within the "Community" section), ModernBride.com can be both useful and entertaining.

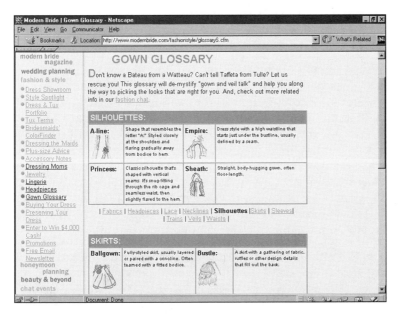

Figure 14.4

ModernBride.com understands that many women coming to the site will be getting married for the first time. This gown glossary is just one of the site's features designed to educate the soon-to-be-new bride.

To the Moon, Alice!

Alice Kramden. Comic foil. Put upon housewife. Role model? Absolutely! In fact, many of the lessons in how to keep a marriage flourishing can be learned by watching episodes of "The Honeymooners," Jackie Gleason's groundbreaking television comedy. As such, no chapter on wedding site would be complete without mentioning `http://www.honeymooners.net`. There you'll find script summaries, audio and video clips, and tons of other information on the classic show. (Please note, this is solely the author's opinion, which might or might not have any basis in reality.)

unGROOM'd

http://www.ungroomed.com

Whereas most Web sites devoted to weddings and marriage are almost unabashedly gynic—devoting at most a subsection of the site to the concerns of the marrying male—unGROOM'd ventures forth to prepare men for marriage (see Figure 14.5). But unlike much of the online wedding information, which is geared towards articles of the how-to variety, unGROOM'd often takes the anecdotal approach. Recent stories held forth on getting married in Las Vegas (penned, unlike other site articles, by a woman), interesting public places to have sex, and what one male's experiences were during his own engagement. Of course the how-to genre is also represented, but instead of a treatise on strategies for dealing with one's in-laws, unGROOM'd gives a stadium by stadium breakdown of people you would need to contact to have a proposal or anniversary flashed on the giant video screen of a sporting event.

Figure 14.5

unGROOM'd prepares the male of the species for marriage.

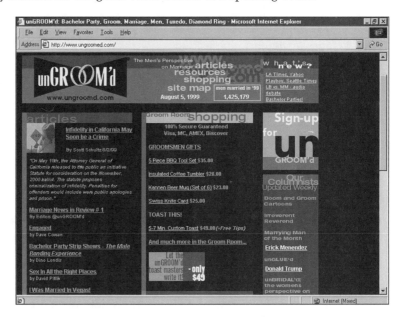

unGROOM'd also offers two services one doesn't readily find on the other sites: You can hire the services of a professional speech writer to whip up the perfect wedding toast and browse the Groom Room—an online store devoted to finding the perfect gifts for your groomsmen. Not to be outdone by the more traditional sites, unGROOM'd also offers a standard wedding registry. One technical issue worth noting is that the Windows version of Netscape Communicator crashed several times while surfing the unGROOM'd site, so using Microsoft Internet Explorer, if available, might be a prudent move.

thebestman.com

http://www.thebestman.com

Although technically a site designed to aid that person who was selected by the groom to stand with him during his last moments of singlehood, thebestman.com has tons of information for soon-to-be-marrieds, as well (see Figure 14.6). Featuring perhaps the Web's best tutorial for making a toast, the site also covers wedding chores including tips for choosing a tuxedo (and a primer for tying a bow tie), suggestions for groomsmen's gifts, and a very nice pictorial guide to diamonds. Of course should the groom be stuck with having to plan his own bachelor party, there is a font of information at thebestman.com. Articles abound on drinkology (how many pints do various keg sizes contain and how does one make that perfect martini?), cigars, and how one deals with what are euphemistically referred to as bachelor party "honeys." The site also is well populated with links to many other Web pages that offer great resources for any wedding-goer and fun quotes from notables discoursing on the various topics covered by the site. Although thebestman.com doesn't cover every wedding planning topic, what it does offer is helpful information in a very fun and winning way.

Figure 14.6

thebestman.com presents wedding-oriented information with testosterone-filled good humor.

Other Sites

As it often does, the Web provides many sites that deal with similar topic matter and the subject of weddings is no exception. The following sites all have similar information to those already mentioned, though they, of course, present it in their own unique way.

Bliss!

http://www.blissezine.com

Bridal Gallery

http://www.bridalgallery.com

iBride

http://www.ibride.com

Wedding Central

http://www.weddingcentral.com

Wedding411.com

http://www.wedding411.com

The Least You Need to Know

➤ The Web provides sites for everything from choosing a wedding gown to picking the song for your first dance as a married couple.

➤ Though weddings are often the bastion of women, sites devoted to preparing a man for marriage also exist.

➤ The Web can be a great tool in distributing wedding information to any size group invited to the affair.

Part 4
I've Had a Hard Day

When a relationship is ending, one can't have too many places to go for support. This section is devoted to Web sites that will assist you with navigating a breakup or divorce, as well as those that just complain about a particular gender. And for those who feel the road to happiness begins with addressing one's own personal issues, there's a chapter offering Web sites devoted to self-help information.

Chapter 15

When a Door Closes, It Gets Dark

In This Chapter

➤ Web sites that help you deal with relationships when they come to an end

➤ Web sites that assist you in coping with divorce

➤ One man's goodbye letter to an ex he never met

Breaking Up Is Hard to Do

Tears. Unresolved feelings. Heartbreak. Such can be the travails of those ending a relationship. But if the Internet got you into this mess, by jingo, the Internet is going to get you out. Welcome to the world of Web sites reaching out to those who know not what to do before, during, or after a relationship dissolves.

Breakup Girl

`http://www.breakupgirl.com`

Breakup Girl, the invention of Lynn Harris and Chris Kalb, uses her vast powers to assist those going through the throes of separation (see Figure 15.1). Each Monday she dispenses advice to the lovelorn always making sure to warn them that she is "a superhero, not a trained psychologist." But although the site's advice column seems to have garnered it the most notoriety, the hidden gem within Breakup Girl is its message board, aptly titled "Deep Dish." If misery loves company, and evidently it does, you will find here an ever-growing community of people grappling with the gamut of relationship-ending issues running from infidelity to what to do with someone's stuff after you're no longer seeing them.

Figure 15.1

Despite the humorous facade, Breakup Girl mixes in support with laughter for those who are going through the pain of a broken relationship.

The site also offers lists of things to do to keep busy (so you're not thinking about that other person), "The Adventures of Breakup Girl" comic (I highly recommend checking out the installment entitled "The Origin of Breakup Girl!"), and multimedia entertainment all geared towards those who want to further explore that place one's heart resides in right after a relationship ends.

Sample Posting from Breakup Girl's Deep Dish Message Board

"Ok. I was just "let go" by the man I'd loved with all of my heart and soul for the last three years. One day out of the blue he tells me he's unhappy with me. So I leave. 2,500 miles away, back to mom's house and job-hunting. It's been almost a month now. He and I still talk a couple of times a week. We're very friendly and animated. We can talk about everything except us.

"But here's the thing, not three weeks after I got here, I met a new guy. A few days after we met we had the most amazing sex.

"Now, I think I'm fairly smart in the ways of relationships and the rebound factor. I'm not looking for a relationship with this guy, nor am I trying to "forget" my recent ex. I'm in this for the amazing sex and the fact that New Guy tells me I'm beautiful on a regular basis. It might be totally surface and completely temporary but it makes me feel good. The thing is, I've never done something so rash like this in my 29 years. EVER. After a major breakup, I've always concentrated on memememe and waited months and months before venturing out again. I thought I was smarter than this, literally jumping into something like this so quickly.

"Here's another facet to this little jewel—New Guy and I had sex (just once) w/out a condom. He pulled out at the last, defining moment. I'm a Pill Gal and he's in the military (Air Force. They have to get checked out like every other month for anything and everything, so I foolishly let him fly w/out a cape). I knew it while I was doing it how utterly STUPID it was. But the thing is, and like I said, I thought I was smarter than this, I want, at this point, so much to believe him that he's OK as far as any germs go.

"I guess what I'm wondering here is, what am I doing? I spend most of my days hoping the ex and I can resolve our issues, and yet I'm having fabulous sex with this very nice, good-looking new guy..... I haven't been able to bring myself to tell the ex about this new guy, and I haven't told the new guy about the recent ex and I feel guilty on both sides because of it.

"I know I must sound completely selfish and immature..... But I'm very confused. My emotions have been up and down so drastically since the ex dropped the bomb. And I'm so dumb, if the ex was doing this, I'd be totally crushed. How come I feel it's ok for me to do this but he can't? How come I'm not using my head? My heart is all over the place getting me into potentially very bad trouble. I don't know what to think or feel anymore."

Seeking Professional Help

The end of a relationship can sometimes trigger or contribute to depression, anger, hopelessness, and other strong emotional reactions. If you are having difficulty coping with life or interacting with others to the extent that your emotions are interfering with your day-to-day existence, you might want to seek professional help. The American Psychological Association (APA) runs an online Help Center at http://helping.apa.org that helps people determine if they need professional psychological assistance; provides guidance in finding a therapist; offers a free brochure that explains what therapy is (which the APA will send you via postal mail); and furnishes articles geared towards helping people cope with a variety of situations.

I Dumped a Loser Society

`http://www.geocities.com/SouthBeach/Cove/9159`

Sometimes ending a relationship is a good thing. A very good thing. And so with that in mind, the I Dumped a Loser Society (IDALS) was born (see Figure 15.2). As IDALS states on its site, it exists "to let everyone know that no matter how big a LOSER their ex is, someone, somewhere, has a bigger loser ex." Though this might seem flippant, the sheer agony on its pages tells a totally different story.

Figure 15.2

IDALS attempts to help people with their breakup misery by revealing how others ended their relationships.

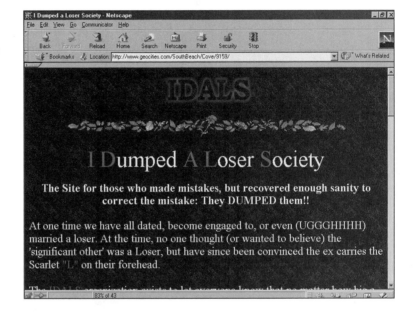

Consisting, as of this writing, of 40 Web pages revealing harrowing tales of abuse, infidelity, and monetary swindling by people's former lovers (as well as your general "bad relationship" stories), IDALS hopes that reading these anecdotes will make people feel better about their own lives.

An IDALS Excerpt

"My loser (thank God he's not MY loser any more) lives in Denver, Colorado and his name is Will. When I first started going out with him, he seemed nice enough. I was stupid enough to lose my virginity to this loser. After we'd been together a while, he started lying to me about any and everything. I really thought I could change him. Then he said he had a "friend" he wanted me to meet. I met his "friend" but it was obvious that they were more than that, the way they hung on each other in front of me. The next day, Will told me that he and his "friend" had a son together. He said he still wanted to be with me & that he loved me but he loved this "friend" a little more cause she'd given him a son. He claimed their relationship was over but about

10 minutes into the conversation he asked if it would be okay if he slept with her while he was still with me. I hacked it off right there. I really didn't believe they had a son, I knew it was a cheap excuse to be w/ two women at the same time. A few weeks ago, my best friend ran into Will. He was with a totally different girl."

True Solitude

Some can't stand to be alone. Others make an uneasy truce with solitude. And still others seek it out. But those who choose to navigate a sailboat around the world without another on board are on a whole other level. To share the true solitude of those who enter the Around Alone race, which pits competitors the world over on a solo 9-month, 30,000 mile journey, surf on over to http://www.aroundalone.com.

Breakup Survival Guides

It would be great if there was a manual that would get all people through the end of relationships under all circumstances. Alas, no such tome exists. That is one of the reasons the advice experts mentioned in Chapter 8, "Advice IS Cheap!" are so popular: people want specific solutions to specific problems. However, there is a commonality to the ending of relationships, so for those who desire some basic all-around advice, the following links provide some.

Relationship Coach Newsletter

http://www.whatittakes.com

(Click the link for "The Library." Then click the link for "The Relationship Coach Newsletter #25.")

Before A Break Up—10 Warning Signs (see Figure 15.3)

10 Ways To Break Up Graciously

10 Ways To Get Over A Break Up

http://www.lovestories.com/ezine/10before.htm

How to Forget Your EX

http://members.tripod.com/forgetyourex/

Figure 15.3

Do you know the warning signs of a relationship that's coming to an end? You can find out what they are at http://www. lovestories.com/ezine/ 10before.htm.

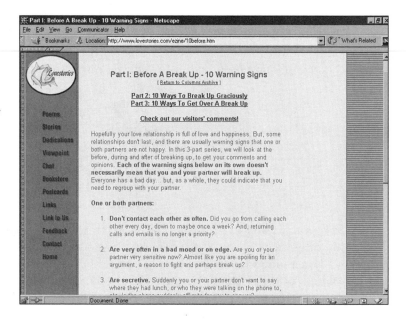

Divorce Survival Sites

As far as breakups go, it doesn't get any worse than divorce. The following sites address almost every divorce-related issue including obtaining a lawyer, handling emotional pain, parenting children through the trauma, alimony, child support, and issues as extreme as child abduction and domestic violence. Each site has its own particularly good aspects. Divorce Central has well populated message boards (referred to as bulletin boards on the site) that supply emotional support and community. divorceinfo.com features depth of subject with more than 100,000 documents available through its speedy text-only presentation. divorcesupport.com offers two divorced advice columns, "Ask the Divorced Guy" and "Ask the Divorced Woman," penned by divorce survivors. And divorcesource.com breaks its information down geographically by state, to allow for variance in divorce law.

Divorce Central (see Figure 15.4)

http://www.divorcecentral.com

divorceinfo.com

http://www.divorceinfo.com

divorcesupport.com

http://www.divorcesupport.com

divorcesource.com

http://www.divorcesource.com

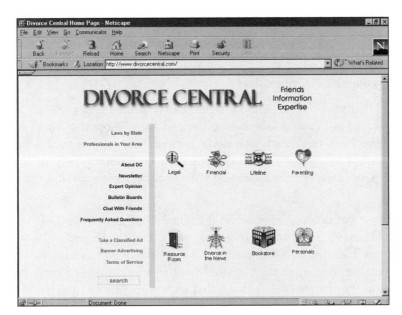

Figure 15.4
Divorce Central is just one of the sites you can go to for help when a marriage ends.

You Lied to Me

Unfortunately, not all romance that begins on the Internet ends well. The following "From the Frontlines" piece is not an anecdote, but the final email that was sent at the end of an 18-month relationship that began online. When contacted for additional information, the writer of the email revealed that during the relationship, he and the woman he loved talked daily by telephone, sent emails, and exchanged photos, presents, and intimate details of their lives. But they never met in person.

The longer time goes on, the easier it gets for me to accept the realization that you've lied to me. I still have not been able to completely discern the facts from the fiction, and I probably never will, but I'm now sure that you could not possibly be what you represented yourself to be.

It still amazes me how you had an answer for everything and how everything seemed to have a bizarre sense of reason behind it. As time has passed though, I've tried to put myself in your shoes and I've realized a couple of things. If I had been in your situation and loved you as much as you'd claimed to love me,

continues

continued

there's no way I would have allowed two months (much less 18) go by without finding a way to be with you. And now, as your excuses have slipped away, my foolishness has just become all the more plain.

I've finally concluded that you must have some other reason for not seeing me and that this reason must have existed long before we were ever "supposed" to get together. Before the New Year's party you never came to; before your medical problems; before all of the lost, misaddressed, or undelivered photos; before you proposed to me (God!); before the cancelled holiday party; before...well, you know the rest.

I should have trusted my gut two years ago when it told me that you were going to break my heart one day. And you have broken my heart, more profoundly than I ever thought possible. Even after all this time, I still have doubts as to whether I will ever be able to love, or trust, again. I have to admit, there's a part of me that hopes you will suffer for having taken that away from me. I'm going to have a difficult time ever forgiving you for what you've done to me. Then again, I suppose that, by this time, my forgiveness probably doesn't mean a whole lot to you anyway.

I suppose the only open issue left is the stuff we each still have that belongs to the other. I have a box all packed up and ready to go but it's too big, too heavy, and not packed in a way that would be suitable for mailing. I thought I would just drop it off on your sister's front porch with a note saying it was for you. I would appreciate you getting my stuff back to me. Most important to me are the pictures I gave you that I don't have any duplicates of. Of lesser importance is the money you owe me. I'm not counting on ever seeing it again though. I've already kind of written it off. I consider it a very expensive—but very valuable—lesson.

I think I've spent way too much time on this note already. Just the fact that I find myself editing and re-editing it to get it "just right" indicates to me that there's still a part of me that's more heavily invested in this than I would like to admit. At least I'm working on it.

I hope you find whatever it is you're really looking for.

—Tom

The Least You Need to Know

➤ The Web offers many sites devoted to helping you survive the end of a relationship.

➤ There also are sites that specialize in assisting people going through a divorce.

There's More to Venting Than Duct Tape

Rule #1: Never Hurt Anyone Who Can Build a Web Page

All the creators of the Web sites in this chapter have been hurt. Hurt by love. Hurt so bad that a book like the one your reading can't make a dent in their damaged psyches. They could have tried to search out their feelings, deal with their anger in a socially acceptable fashion, or seek professional help. Perhaps they even did, but what's really important is that they channeled all their anger into entertaining and educating those who might follow their disastrous path through the eddies of love.

Heartless Bitches International

`http://www.heartless-bitches.com`

There is something quite fulfilling about watching an animated ax chopping repeatedly into a blood-spurting heart. But this is only one of the many pleasures accessible to those who visit the Heartless Bitches International site (see Figure 16.1). Rife with pungent satire (and sometimes just plain anger) the site's many features include The Sappy Site of the Week (which links to and skewers a site the writer finds particularly offensive) and many rants against everything from "pop-psychology morons" to "people who precede every sneeze with a loud yelp."

Figure 16.1

Alas, not every Web site has a manifesto, but luckily Heartless Bitches International does and displays it proudly.

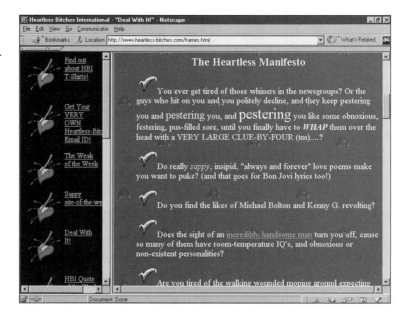

Many of the heartless bitches (they do refer to themselves this way) who belong to the site have posted essays explaining why they are a heartless bitch. "I have no tolerance for men that are intimidated because I am blond and have a brain. Suddenly, I am not likeable material. What, you have to be an idiot to get a date in the real world?" asks Denise in one of the more PG-rated entries.

Those who consider themselves a heartless bitch can apply for membership at the site by filling out a Web form, printing it out, and submitting the completed application via postal mail. Be sure to read the site's manifesto and "Heartless Hints to the Hopeful" because if your application is rejected your submission could wind up in the site's "The Weak of the Week" section, which mercilessly mocks those applicants who just don't measure up to Heartless Bitch standards. Those who are accepted as members gain admission to the site's private message board and receive a nifty membership ID card.

Brotherhood of Eternal Bachelors

`http://www.geocities.com/CollegePark/5923/beb.html`

If you belong to that segment of the population not inclined to join Heartless Bitches International, you might want to check out the Brotherhood of Eternal Bachelors (see

Figure 16.2). Though not as thoroughly mean-spirited as the Heartless Bitches, the brotherhood does get its occasional licks in with such entries as commandment number seven of the brotherhood's Ten Commandments, which states "Thou holdest the sacred right to secretly compare thy Ex's new boyfriend TO many species of weasles [sic]."

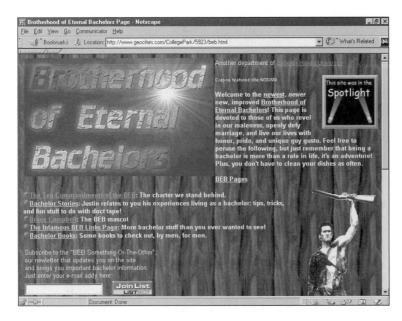

Figure 16.2

Welcome to The Brotherhood of Eternal Bachelors Web site with its official mascot, actor Bruce Campbell of the "Evil Dead" movies, pictured in the lower-right corner.

Although there is no official ID card, you can subscribe to the site's free newsletter that will update you on important bachelor information, as well as enjoy it's articles, which include an explanation of why actor Bruce Campbell of the "Evil Dead" movies was selected as the brotherhood's mascot.

Joelogon's Foolproof Guide to Making Any Woman Your Platonic Friend

`http://www.wizard.net/~joelogon/platonic`

If you're a woman, you might surf over to Joelogon's Foolproof Guide to Making Any Woman Your Platonic Friend and think it was a somewhat bitter, yet humorous site.

Where Is the Love?

Those with extra bile to spew aren't limiting themselves to mere gender bashing. Just type the word "hate" into any search engine and you'll be bombarded by sites devoted to ranting against everything from mayonnaise (`http://www.nomayo.com`) to Microsoft (`http://www.tstonramp.com/~freiheit/antim$.shtml`).

However, if you're a man who's gone through the experience of having a woman tell you "I just want to be friends," this site will speak to you more deeply than the collected works of the Western canon.

Employing a "how-to" approach, the guide examines "the tendency of women to develop close friendships with their male acquaintances, thereby preemptively eliminating any possibility of a romantic relationship, the result of which is to remove the poor schmuck's heart and shred it." Content within the guide includes the "do's and don'ts of cultivating and maintaining a platonic friendship with a woman you would otherwise want to have a relationship with and quite possibly marry" as well as "the care and feeding of your platonic friend" and a list of excuses women make for not going out with men they claim to find attractive in some way. Topping off the site is a section entitled "Excess Bitterness" in which readers of the site share their own experiences with women who didn't look at them in a romantic way. And for those who'd like to contribute their own bile, there's a convenient link to an email address.

Chicks Suck

http://chickssuck.shutdown.com

There's generalized anger. Anger against society. Even self-aimed anger. But when it becomes personal, that's when things become really interesting. Welcome to the world of Chicks Suck, where the author regales all who traverse these black pages with tales designed to amplify the premise of the site's title. It seems the site's creator has had trouble finding women willing to have sex with him (though, as of this writing, he's posted his thoughts on the woman he's now "committed" to). As such he holds forth in amusing detail all the experiences he has had with women that have been less than satisfactory. The site has become so popular that it features a FAQs (Frequently Asked Questions) page (see Figure 16.3) that answers such questions as why the site's author doesn't just meet chicks on the Internet ("Internet chat rooms are evil") and amplifies on his attitude with statements like "Guys suck less than chicks though, because we're simple. We want sex. Most chicks don't know what they want." Along with the author's many tales of inter-gender interaction (including a lengthy discourse on the relationship he is now embroiled in) are pages devoted to the hate mail and nice mail he's received, as well as rants on various topics including circumcision and Valentines Day.

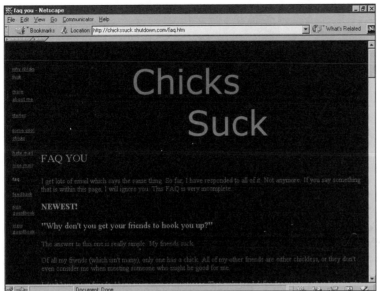

Figure 16.3

Everything you ever wanted to know about the Chicks Suck site can be found in the "FAQ YOU" page.

bitterslut

http://www.bitterslut.com

bitterslut, as the name suggests, is almost entirely comprised of the rantings, musings, and responses of women who have been emotionally hurt by others. With message boards featuring titles like bitterchat, vengeful acts, and bitter libel, those who frequent the site are encouraged to donate as much spleen as humanly possible. Upon a recent visit to the vengeful acts bulletin board I learned some really good techniques for getting back at one's ex-lover including using a squirt bottle of Miracle Grow to leave a creative message via your victim's lawn that's "lush, green, and healthy." Though I have no empirical data supporting whether this or any of the other suggestions offered on the site work, reading bittersluts made me wonder if these women had ever dated the male authors of Chicks Suck or Girls? Ugh!

She Knows What She Wants

I was in a chat room when I got an instant message from someone, who immediately asked, "M or F?" I never would answer this question outright, because I liked the anonymity of gender that chat rooms and instant messaging provided. I must have eventually told him I was a female, and he asked me if I had ever had cybersex, to which I honestly replied "no." He then launched into what I assume was his idea of cyber-foreplay, telling me something about how he was pulling my panties down, etc, etc. I certainly could have told him to go to hell, or signed off, or done any number of things, but I admit I was interested. Not necessarily in participating, but in at least seeing how far he was going to go with this. And I was also interested in whether this would be at all titillating to me, as I had heard about cybersex and could never imagie what the appeal was.

I can't really remember how the exchange ended. I did eventually contribute a bit to the action, but certainly not as whole-heartedly as he. And I wasn't the slightest bit aroused. But when he emailed me the next day, I did return the email, and we chatted online again soon after. It was then that he came out with the fact that he was in a relationship, lived with his girlfriend, and that she was asleep in the next room as he had been typing all of this pornographic stuff to me. I reasoned with him about the moral implications of this, but he said there was no harm in just talking about it. But then I got the impression he was definitely into fooling around on her. By this time we discovered we had quite a bit in common so I kept in contact with him through email, even though I knew this guy was obviously an untrustworthy dog.

Within a couple of weeks, he started saying he wanted to meet. I resisted, reminding him of his girlfriend. That didn't deter him. I finally decided to give in to my curiosity (I was dying to know what this guy looked like) and meet up with him, even though I knew there was no way I would ever get involved with him in any way, shape, or form.

I named the place we'd meet at for lunch and I fabricated an appointment to go to afterwards so that I would have a reason for escape if I needed it. I also arrived early so he wouldn't see which direction I came from, in case he tried to figure out where I lived.

continues

continued

When he arrived I immediately thought this was not someone to whom I would be attracted. While he wasn't unattractive, he was not at all my type. But, I thought, it will be interesting to have lunch with him, and then I never have to see him again.

This guy immediately showed himself to be a depressing, weak, shlump. He didn't take any initiative in ordering food, in conversation, in ANYTHING. Mostly what he talked about the entire time is how his mother had died a few weeks before. What I was supposed to do to console this stranger who was obviously in mourning, and never should have been there with me in the first place, was beyond me. After I said, "Gosh, that's terrible, I'm so sorry for your loss" about 15 times, I didn't know what to say anymore. Thankfully, the service was quick, we finished, I made my appointment excuse, and beat a quick retreat, walking the opposite way from my apartment so he couldn't follow me.

I thought I had been polite, but certainly less than enthusiastic, so that he would perhaps get the picture that I was not interested. But he emailed me the next day saying what a fabulous time he had and that he wanted to see me again. I emailed back a very nice, but firm, reply that I wasn't interested and I never heard from him again.

—Morgan

Application to Be My Ex-Boyfriend

`http://www.tigergirl.com/cyberslut/boyfriend`

Cheryl Thompson, or tigergirl as some know her, has decided to dispense with the usual brouhaha of dating. There's no need to converse, have dinner, meet each other's relatives, or share any experiences on the road to ending your relationship with her. Instead, just fill out the handy Web form and you (whether you be male or female) can apply to be her ex-boyfriend (see Figure 16.4). There are no prizes (though she does sometimes link people's Web sites to hers), but are there ever any when a relationship ends?

Figure 16.4

A portion of "The Application to Be My Ex-Boyfriend" with some sample answers filled in.

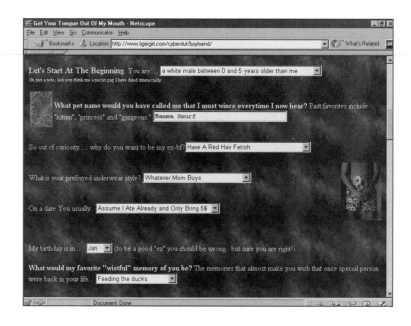

Girls? Ugh!

http://www.netcomuk.co.uk/~tcant/Ugh/index.html

Nothing describes the philosophy of Girls! Ugh!, "The Official Website of Not Having a Girlfriend," better than the site's opening paragraph which states "Women. They may seem cute and harmless, but underneath their cuddly exteriors lies a cold calculating thing. Like a bunny rabbit that is actually a robot in a bunny rabbit suit. Sort of. This page's DEDICATED MISSION is to help poor fools like yourself avoid becoming trapped in the most sinister of all a woman's schemes...A RELATIONSHIP." In service to this mission the site offers up articles that explain why having a girlfriend is bad, simple tactics to avoid obtaining a girlfriend, and why photographs of women are superior to the real thing. Also of use to those wanting to compare their misery to others is a catalog of the worst lines people have used to end a relationship.

Men Suck

http://www.mensuck.org

Is it a focal point for women's anger towards men? An instructional guide in the ways of carnal pleasure? A giant goof on the battle of the sexes? Men Suck is all of these and more. Often using colorful language (as do many of the sites in this chapter), the site's creator, Jaime, offers all manner of information. This information includes 40 ways men fail in bed (see Figure 16.5), why the men she's dated (excluding her current boyfriend) suck, and serious instructional articles on the proper way to sexually pleasure various parts of the female and male anatomy. A Submit-a-Jerk page allows you to post your own man-sucking tale, Stupid Men Jokes offer a comic take on gender differences, and a message board lets surfers offer up their own opinions.

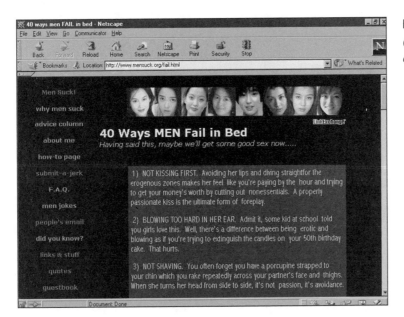

Figure 16.5
One of the informative articles from Men Suck.

The Least You Need to Know

➤ Success might be the best revenge, but many people have not counted out the joy of creating a Web page to humiliate former lovers in public.

➤ Both men and women have specific complaints about the opposite sex.

➤ Anger is as common on the Web as HTML code.

Chapter 17

Me, Myself, and I

In This Chapter

➤ Web sites concentrated on assisting you with personal growth

➤ Web sites designed to help you solve problems and set goals

➤ A Web site geared towards personal growth through dream interpretation

---

If I Use the Web, Is It Really Self-Help?

Flight attendants are always quick to point out that in an emergency, when traveling with a child by plane, you should always put on your own oxygen mask before placing one on the child's head. This makes perfect sense, for if you lost consciousness while assisting the child, one or both of you could die. Many of the world's great thinkers have felt the same way about relationships: The more you develop and grow as an individual prior to entering a relationship, the better you will be able to deal with interpersonal emergencies. As such, the following Web sites are devoted to personal growth.

SELF-Therapy

`http://www.execpc.com/~tonyz`

Each page of the SELF-Therapy Web site ends with the words "Enjoy Your Changes!" for that is what the site hopes to facilitate you to do (see Figure 17.1). Authored by psychotherapist Tony Schirtzinger, the site is divided into nine major topic areas, including The Biggies (Guidelines for Emotional Health, About Change, and so on); Couples & Relationships (Most Common Relationship Problems, How Happy Couples Stay That Way, and so on); and Depression, Anger & Guilt (Depression: What to Do About It, and so on).

Figure 17.1

The SELF-Therapy site has many introspective tools, such as this Other Signs of Emotional Health Checklist.

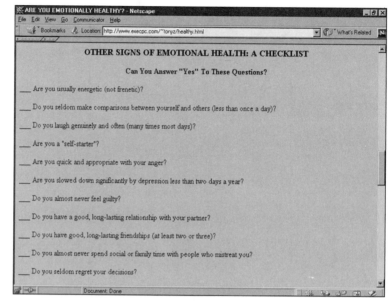

Using a mixture of checklists, advice, and tools for self-examination (such as questions to ask yourself), the site assists readers with various life-problems. At the same time it is quick to post the disclaimer that "This site is not for everyone and nothing here is an acceptable substitute for good face-to-face therapy if you need it." However, for those who have a hankering to probe their own feelings, SELF-Therapy provides some useful suggestions for how to go about it.

Be Your Own Therapist

`http://www.psychologyhelp.com/book.shtml`

Believing that "More than 90% of the work in effective therapy is done OUTSIDE the therapy hour," Thayer White, a marriage, family, and child counselor with a master's degree in Transpersonal Counseling Psychology, has written the book *Be Your Own Therapist* and posted it online (see Figure 17.2). In a straightforward manner, White equates people with houses that are fixer-uppers, "structurally sound but showing needs for a variety of repairs." These repairs are of course the personal growth areas that the book addresses, and address them it does covering a huge swath of territory including thinking and cognitive processes, emotions, the roots of trauma, spirituality, male and female misconceptions, and family issues among many others. Though

White covers some material you might not expect, such as his beliefs concerning the connection between food allergies and mental health, the site features a wealth of material for those working on personal issues.

Test Subject: You

Not every person will want to treat every problem he or she has as an in-depth self-exploratory project. That's why self-help quizzes have become so popular. They allow people the chance to take their pulse on a variety of issues before deciding whether or not a deeper personal examination is necessary. A good place to take these quizzes online is http://www.psychtests.com. The site features tests examining your relationships, intelligence, emotional health, personality, and career. There's even a leadership test. And most importantly, all quizzes are scored automatically by the site with a detailed analysis of the results delivered right to your screen.

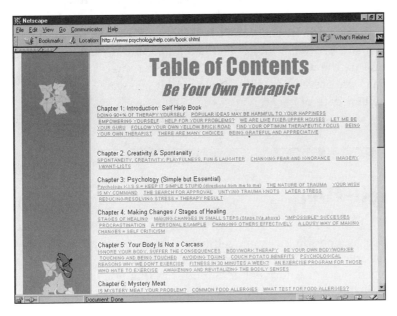

Figure 17.2

The Table of Contents to Be Your Own Therapist.

Good Company

I met Steve online when he replied to my personal ad. Fortunately, or unfortunately, I had started to date another guy who had responded to the same ad just a few weeks before. Knowing that I was entering a relationship with this other man, I told Steve I had just met someone. But he was so engaging, funny, and down-to-earth that we started to correspond as friends.

Sure enough, two months later the other guy and I realize that it's not working out and call it quits. However, when I tell Steve, he starts acting aloof. Though he claimed he still wasn't dating anyone else, he said it didn't "feel right" to meet yet. Normally, I would probably just walk away, but I loved talking to him so much (we had begun having phone conversations) that I thought I'd give it a little more time.

A couple of weeks later he asked me to dinner. Nervous as a high school girl going to the prom, I must have changed clothes 20 times that night before I felt sexy. When I got to the restaurant, the reservation was there but Steve wasn't. After 45 minutes I knew he wasn't going to come. I was crushed. I was furious. My head was swimming. And every 10 minutes the maitre d' was telling me he really couldn't hold my table any longer. I don't know where I got the nerve, but I went into that restaurant, ordered a lobster and had a sumptuous meal. I gave huge tips to the maitre d', the waiter, and the sommelier. And when I got home that evening, an email from Steve was waiting for me. All it said was "Sorry." But I wasn't. I had had the best date of my life.

—*Susan*

Psychological Self-Help

`http://mentalhelp.net/psyhelp`

Half of the battle to grow as a person, say some self-help experts, is identifying what it is you want to change about yourself. If you are one of those people who already has a good idea of the behaviors or emotional underpinnings that you'd like to alter, then Psychological Self-Help might be a good site to check out (see Figure 17.3). Another book posted to the Web, *Psychological Self-Help*, was written by Dr. Clayton E. Tucker-Ladd, a clinical psychologist, who starts off his tome by defining self-help as "intentional coping." From there he starts outlining his basic approach to tackling self-help projects, which begins with understanding the different parts to each problem: behavior involved, emotions experienced, skills needed, mental processes involved, and unconscious forces that might contribute to your problems. He then outlines a 10-step approach to completing self-help projects. But the bulk of the book deals with explaining the emotional forces at work within people. As such, Dr. Tucker-Ladd features chapters on depression and self-concept; anger and aggression; dependency and conformity; and dating, love, marriage, and sex, among other topics.

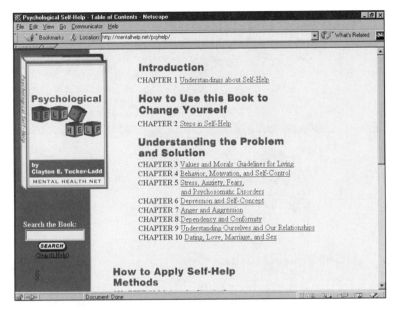

Figure 17.3

The table of contents to Psychological Self-Help.

Mind Tools

`http://www.mindtools.com`

Mind Tools was designed for those who eschew the touchy-feely approach to personal growth (see Figure 17.4). In fact, none of the content deals with emotions in any way, instead concentrating on developing skills to assist you to think more clearly and productively.

The Mind Tools site features in-depth articles about problem solving, retaining information, improving memory, and managing stress. In addition, it features tons of information on time management, setting goals, and communication skills. And for the athlete looking to get a competitive mental edge, Mind Tools also offers a section of the site devoted to sports psychology.

Figure 17.4

Mind Tools helps you build skills, as opposed to managing your emotions, to create a better life for yourself.

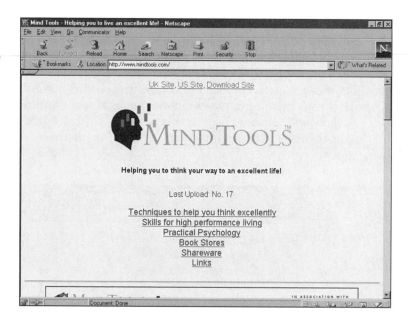

Get Your ANGRIES Out

Although the sites mentioned in this chapter are, for the most part, general self-help sites that offer assistance with many problems, the Web also provides sites that specialize in giving you the tools to attack a particular problem. A good example of this is the Get Your ANGRIES Out site at `http://members.aol.com/AngriesOut`. In more than three dozen articles, the site addresses ways that adults, children, and teachers can deal with anger in a healthy and responsible way. In addition, ANGRIES Out provides many links to other sites that help children and adults deal with anger and other problems.

Goal Map

`http://www.goalmap.com`

What do you want out of life in the next 12 months? If you're having trouble answering that question, or you just want to crystallize your thought processes to help you achieve your desires, then Goal Map might be what you're looking for. The free service guides users through a process that takes approximately 30 minutes, after which a visual representation of what you want to achieve over the next year is created. In what Goal Map calls The Discovery Phase (see Figure 17.5), users answer a series of multiple choice questions divided into four categories: Self & Wellbeing, Business & Career, Home & Family, and Community & Humanity. After refining your answers until you compose small word capsules defining your goals, the site moves you onto the Design Phase that lets you assign an icon to each goal you've targeted. Upon registering with the site, which is also free, you get to save your map online for future reference and use Goal Map's Goal Enablement Tool, which allows you to define how to achieve each particular objective.

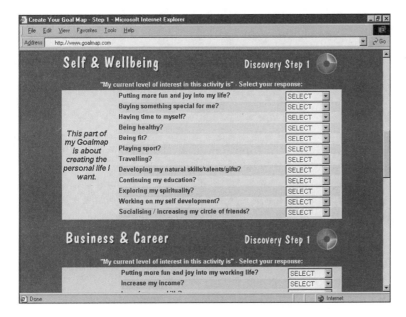

Figure 17.5

The first step in Goal Map's Discovery Phase is answering multiple choice questions from different categories.

Temple of Dreams

`http://www.templeofdreams.com`

"The guides, gurus, and gods who can truly help us understand who we are and what we need and where we should go and how to get there dwell within us. They reside in that thoroughly magical world that we visit every night—the extraordinary and unpredictable, mysterious and revelatory, unexplored world of our dreams." Citing this philosophy, former television writers Lane Sarasohn and his wife Carol have put Temple of Dreams on the Web to help people seek personal growth via dream interpretation (see Figure 17.6).

Figure 17.6

How can your dreams help you grow as a person? Perhaps the Temple of Dreams has the answer.

Those looking for quick answers of the type found in books about the symbolism of objects and events in dreams are probably best served someplace else. The site's "Teachings" section offers a preface and 10 lessons that provide a general framework for you to begin the process of examining the tapestry of thought comprising a dream. Also featured on the site are actual dreams people have had (each accompanied by an interpretation), essays, dream-related articles, and quotations about dreams. For those interested in examining the world they inhabit during sleep, Temple of Dreams might make a good starting point.

Other Mental Health Issues

Although the previous sites all deal with personal growth, there are many areas of mental health that they do not address. These include, but are not limited to, addiction, abuse, trauma, physical and mental handicaps, disease, and eating disorders. As there are many offline, as well as online, resources for assisting people in dealing with these problems (as well as many others not mentioned here), these topics are best served elsewhere.

The Least You Need to Know

➤ The Web contains sites designed to help you with personal growth via dealing with your emotions or by building skills in such areas as setting goals and problem solving.

➤ There are also Web-based resources for solving personal problems using less conventional methods, such as dream interpretation.

Part 5

Has Anyone Seen My Magic Eight Ball?

They say that no one knows the future, but is that really true? This final part of The Complete Idiot's Guide to Online Dating and Relating *looks at Web sites that try to predict your future, romantically or otherwise. As an added bonus, this book's author also weighs in with his predictions for the future of online dating and relating.*

Chapter 18

"I See a Tall, Dark, and Handsome..."

In This Chapter

➤ Web sites that try to help you predict your future, romantic or otherwise, via astrology, runes, Tarot, and other methods

➤ Web sites that parody the sites trying to help you predict your future

Serious Futures

When will I meet someone I like? When will I be married? Will I ever obtain any fashion sense? Ah, the myriad questions people looking to meet others want answered. Fortunately, there's no end to the Web resources willing to predict your future, romantically or otherwise.

Astronet

http://www.astronet.com

Anyone can create a Web site that alleges to foretell the future, as do the dozens of horoscope sites on the Web. But how many sites claim to have a Psychic Love Doctor on call? That, my friends, would only be Astronet (see Figure 18.1). The Psychic Love Doctor, a.k.a. Deborah Leigh, has been "studying the principles of personal prophesy for the past 14 years." Although the site doesn't teach you to perceive the future by reading ordinary playing cards, as Ms. Leigh does, it does have articles penned by her explaining how the cards can guide you. In addition to this service, Astronet has many horoscope choices including LoveScopes, ErotiScopes, and PassionScopes, in addition to your sign's daily horoscope. There is even something called "The Daily Muffin," though I'm afraid to say that that feature lost me with phrases like "the Sun at 17 degrees of Leo sits at a harsh square to restrictive Saturn in Taurus." Though Astronet supplies these and other services for free, be aware that certain site features, like personal astrological readings, are fee-based.

Figure 18.1

Get your "Daily Muffin" and so much more at Astronet.

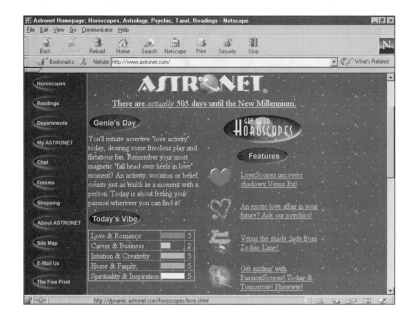

According to Astronet, "more than 50 million people (approximately 37% of adult Americans) say they believe in or use horoscopes and astrology regularly to gain an edge in their lives and decisions." There's no doubt that a goodly portion of these people get their information from Astronet, because the site also syndicates its Web content to other well-traveled astrology bastions like Yahoo! Astrology.

Rob Brezsny's Real Astrology

http://www.realastrology.com

Put succinctly, Rob Brezsny gives good horoscope. On his best days he's insightful, prodding, and entertaining. On his worst days he's just damn funny. His Real Astrology, a staple of alternative news weeklies for more than a decade, should be a don't miss on each Wednesday it's posted on the Web (see Figure 18.2). For those unfamiliar with his horoscopes, the following should give you a good idea of his writing style.

Be Careful with Your Money

The future is big business. Some Web sites will offer to sell you services such as psychic readings and natal charting for fees that range from a token payment to several hundred dollars. Practice extreme caution if you plan to purchase any astrological or psychic goods or services via the Web. This is one area of online commerce that unfortunately has many who would take your money and give little in return.

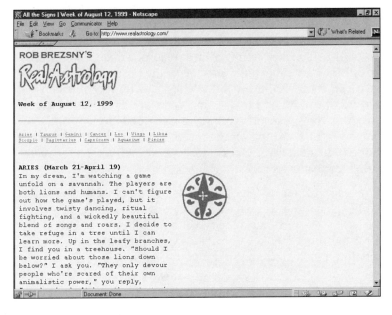

Figure 18.2

Rob Brezsny's Real Astrology gives good horoscope.

Excerpt from Rob Brezsny's Real Astrology

"I'm having pangs of guilt about how relentlessly meaningful I've been lately. To atone, I'll brag about two lessons I learned recently while in the company of a couple of eight-year-old girls. 1) It's quite fun to smash your fist down on unopened bags of potato chips lying on a table, thereby creating a loud pop and sending a spray of crumbs out one end. 2) The maximum amount you can let a string of snot droop down out of your nose, and then suck it back up is 14 inches. There you have it, Capricorn. If you know what's good for you, you'll follow my silly example. Get out and correct for your own excessive gravity."

Tarot Magic

http://www.tarotmagic.com

I have to admit I like my future foretold without a lot of research on my part. As such I never really investigated Tarot cards with all their meanings and interpretations. But the Tarot Magic Web site definitely makes getting a Tarot reading (albeit a simplified one) fun while providing all the card's meanings specific to the position they are dealt. Visitors to the site get to choose from the Rider-Waite and Tarot of the Stars decks. After typing in a word or two about the question you want to ask and deciding on a one or three card reading, the site displays a fanned face-down deck of cards. By clicking the fan, cards are dealt into position on the screen (see Figure 18.3). After all the cards are dealt, clicking individual cards takes you to a new Web page to explain the meaning of the reading for that card.

In addition to performing readings, Tarot Magic also contains a library of every Tarot card used on the site with explanations of each card's meaning. In this way, if you do readings with an offline deck, you can still use the site as a reference tool. Although the purpose of the site is ostensibly to sell a Tarot CD-ROM product, Tarot Magic still provides a fun and entertaining look at the mysteries of the Tarot.

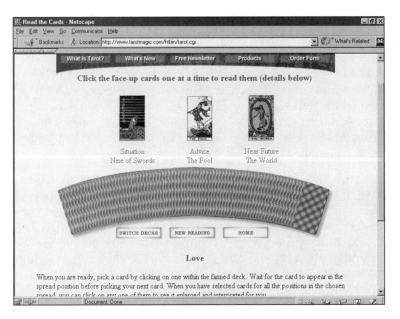

Figure 18.3

A reading provided by Tarot Magic's Web site.

Faith in Computers

Dating rituals are pretty much the same online as they are in the real world. Most of the time the guy has to be the aggressor and contact the woman, who then decides if she's interested. So you can imagine my surprise when after several weeks I received an answer to my online personal.

At first, I was pretty excited. After all, who doesn't want to be pursued. But things got weird fairly quickly. Evidently this woman wasn't only interested, but was convinced that I was her "soul mate." She had run some feature on the matchmaking site that matched her to compatible men, and I was the only one out of thousands that she was a match for. The first day that she wrote me I got two emails. The second day three. They pretty much all said the same thing: "We are destined to be together" and "The computer matched us, so you must be the one!" I informed her as politely as I could that I wasn't interested. She took the hint after about a week.

—Phil

Facade

`http://www.facade.com`

Like the Tarot Magic Web site, Facade offers interactive Tarot readings. It also delves into the future with readings from runes (materials found in nature inscribed with Norse letters), the I Ching (coins that are cast or yarrow sticks that are divided and then referenced for interpretation in Confucius' *Book of Changes*), Stichomancy (reading a random passage from any book while concentrating on a topic that requires further enlightenment), and Bibliomancy (Stichomancy using the King James Bible).

Within many of the site's sections you can become more specific in your exploration of the future. In the runes section you can choose the Runes of Black for questions regarding spiritual matters, the Runes of Gold for queries pertaining to material prosperity, the Runes of Jade for predictions of physical well-being, and the Runes of Stone for pondering relationships with others (see Figure 18.4). The Tarot section features readings from seven different decks and card spreads in your choice of four different arrangements. And the I Ching portion of the site offers you the choice to cast coins or divide the yarrow. For those both new and familiar with these divination techniques, the site makes for a fun and educational visit.

Figure 18.4

A rune reading from the Facade Web site.

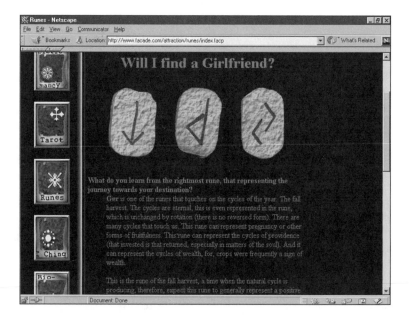

Not So Serious Futures

Not everyone believes in the ability to predict the future. As such, some have taken the time to create Web sites that mock the sites that do. If you feel all this glimpsing into the future is a bunch of hooey (and maybe even if you don't), these sites might be up your astral alley.

Dean Martin's Sunny Summertime Horoscopes

`http://www.word.com/gigo/daron_dean/dean1.html`

Dean Martin.. He was suave. Composed. A ladies man who could charm his escort or joke around with the guys without spilling a drop of his martini. But could he predict the future? Evidently so, as Daron Murphy has successfully channeled Dean's spirit to provide this Web site's look into the future (see Figure 18.5). With swingin' advice like "sometimes the chips come in for the cat who keeps it cool" one can't go too wrong following Deano's predictions.

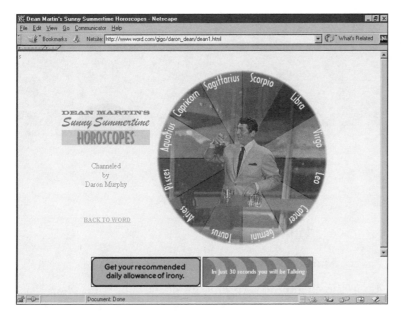

Figure 18.5

Deano sees the future and it's swingin'!

Foo Foo's Cat Astrology

`http://www.nucleus.com/~howiet/foofoo`

Foo Foo, a white domestic short hair, has been blessed with extraordinary powers. According to his bio on the Foo Foo's Cat Astrology Web site (see Figure 18.6), "as a kitten, he was able to predict when a hairball would be coughed up just from the patterns in his litter box." As a result of these gifts, a degree from Oxford and the study of Sufi mysticism, Foo Foo can use astrology to predict your cat's future or personality traits. For instance, owners of Aries cats should get used to retrieving them from the pound as Aries is the sign of wanderlust. Other informative features of the site include a chart to see if you and your cat are astrologically compatible and a diagram that shows how the astrological signs govern different parts of your cat's anatomy.

Figure 18.6

Foo Foo is an expert in cat astrology.

Many Futures Await

Not nearly enough sites in this chapter to sate your astrological appetite? Have no fear, for Astropro's Web site of the Week (http://www.astropro.com/ wow-logs.html) brings to light a new natal Web wonder each week. In addition, Astropro maintains an archive of links to more than 150 sites it has featured since 1996. Most of the featured Web addresses tend to approach the art of astrology seriously, but the site's creator, Richard Nolle, does focus on the occasional humorous astrology destination. One of the fun ones he featured in the summer of 1999 was the Horoscope-O-Matic found at http://www.intoon.com/ horoscope.html. You'll need the Shockwave plug-in for your browser (download-able from the site if you don't already have it) to view your horoscope, but it's worth the trouble to enjoy advice like "Heroism causes others to admire you. Capitalize on that. Lead them to true enlightenment through sword swallowing."

Magic 8-Balls Unlimited

Sometimes nothing other than immediate gratification will do ("I need to know my future and I need to know it NOW!"). Well, fear not, for the majority of online predictors are of the Magic 8-Ball variety: you ask a yes or no question, and with a single click of your mouse a Web page appears with your future neatly laid out. There are dozens of these sites, so I have listed four that hopefully will serve most people's needs quite adequately.

The first one, The Magic 8-Ball, is a recreation of the offline Tyco novelty that has been popular for years. It even displays its predictions on a triangular surface peering beneath the 8-Ball's famous blue liquid. Floaty Oracle foresees the future by displaying a pen with a ball that floats to either the word "YES" or the word "NO." Kurt Cobain's Magic Talking 8-Ball (see Figure 18.7) uses sound clips of the dead musician's voice to deliver the Nirvana frontman's predictions from the next world. And The Magic 8-Ball Unofficial Home Page has links to many of the other 8-Ball like pages that can be found around the Web. The Unofficial Home Page also features a fascinating article (accompanied by detailed photographs) showing the dissection of an actual Magic 8-Ball for those who have always wondered where its miraculous powers come from.

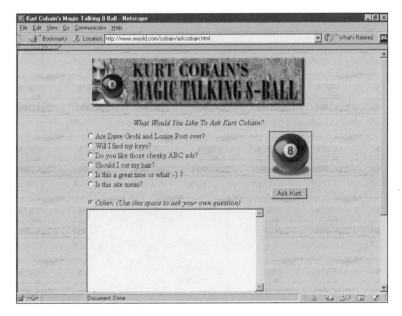

Figure 18.7

Kurt Cobain's Magic Talking 8-Ball will reveal your future in the musician's own voice.

The Magic 8-Ball

http://www.springfield-il.com/kids/8ball/8_ball.html

Floaty Oracle

`http://www.floaty.com/oracle`

Kurt Cobain's Magic Talking 8-Ball

`http://www.xworld.com/cobain/askcobain.html`

The Magic 8-Ball—An Unofficial Home Page

`http://ofb.net/8ball`

The Least You Need to Know

➤ Plenty of Web sites exist for those wanting to explore astrology, Tarot, runes, and other methods for predicting the future.

➤ Plenty of Web sites exist for those wanting to have a good laugh as a result of mock attempts to predict the future.

Chapter 19

Listen to Me!
Listen to Me!

The Idiot's Guide's Predictions for the Future of Dating and Relating Online

Where will online dating and relating be in 50 years? Here are some predictions.

1. Instead of scanned photos, long-distance honeys now exchange three-dimensional holographs by email. However, due to an unfortunate bug in Outlook 2050, some people see their loved one's face replaced by that of a dog. Microsoft Chairman Bill Gates IV, states that the problem is due to the presence of Animals 2050, programming which allows any creature from an ant to an orangutan to input simple commands into Windows.

2. An odd anti-Web movement has overtaken some online socializers. As a result, many have resurrected the practice of placing personal ads in, of all things, magazines. Since the only magazine still publishing is AOL's *You've Got Tales!*, this monthly has become the de facto personals vehicle. However, so that people will actually read the ad, those who place printed personals are forced to advertise them on the Web.

3. Chat rooms where people exchange emotions have become so popular that a huge black market catering to those who hide their online gender sells stolen feelings.

4. To save time, many corporate executives now have instant messages beamed directly to their brains. Playful hackers have devised a way to stimulate a person's taste buds to make these messages leave the taste of SPAM.

5. Due to a discovery 20 years earlier that computer mice would actually work better if replaced with real rodents, the common field mouse has now been added to the list of endangered species. This has become such a divisive issue that personal ads, along with such staples as gender, body type, and religious preference, now list a choice for "fur or plastic."

6. Jack and Suzanne Perlman, the first couple married over the Internet, celebrate their 45th wedding anniversary. The last time they were physically in the same room was for their twentieth. "It just wasn't for us," explains Jack.

7. Sensors that attach to computer mice allow people who meet in chat rooms to have the experience of holding hands. Unfortunately, hospital emergency rooms get visits daily from those who've suffered third degree burns as a result of attaching the devices to other body parts.

8. *The New York Times on the Web*'s nonfiction bestseller list is headed by two titles: "Go from Online to On Fire" and "Chat Your Way to a Slimmer You."

9. Cyber-dating now allows a couple to have dinner, see a movie, and spend an entire evening together while being thousands of miles apart. "I didn't like it," complained one woman. "He was so involved with his own computer, he hardly noticed mine."

10. Mothers Against CyberSex (MACS) is founded. This fringe group claims people should practice the real thing.

Index

Y-Z

She's got a computer, but it's no fun. The solution?

The Perfect Date™

A CD-ROM for women who have Windows 95/98

We've all been there. You go out on a blind date, which turns out so mismatched and awful that months later you're laughing hysterically at how preposterous the whole thing was. Well, now you can skip the horrifying "live through it" stage and go right to the fun with The Perfect Date™, an interactive novelty on CD-ROM for women who have a computer running Windows 95/98.

Rendered in beautiful watercolor illustrations, The Perfect Date™ begins when you meet your date at a restaurant and find yourself in conversation with a man (and we use that term loosely) who, depending on the questions you ask, puts his personalities right on display. Mamma's Boy, Sugar Daddy, Punk Rocker—all of these and more does he become as he tries his dysfunctional best to win your heart. Also along for the ride are your waiter and the restaurant's patrons, which include the local drunk and a lady advisor (should you need help relating to your dinner companion).

Give The Perfect Date™ to a friend or go on The Perfect Date™ yourself! All copies come with a 30-day money-back guarantee!

Three ways to purchase The Perfect Date™

1. Order online at www.size-eight.com

   Free shipping and handling for online orders means you get The Perfect Date™ for only $14.95 per copy!

2. Fax the coupon below to (603) 994-4725

   Each copy costs $17.95, which includes a $3 s/h fee.

3. Mail the coupon below to Size Eight Software

   Each copy costs $17.95, which includes a $3 s/h fee.

To order The Perfect Date™ (@ $17.95/copy), mail this coupon to: Size Eight Software, Cherokee Station, P.O. Box 20735, New York, NY 10021-0074. We cannot accept cash or personal checks. Please allow two to three weeks for delivery.

Payment Method: _____ Visa _____ MasterCard _____ American Express _____ Money Order

Credit Card #: _____ Number of copies ordered: _____

For credit card payment, authorize with your signature: _____

Name _____ Email address _____

Address _____

City _____ State _____ Zip Code _____

Minimum system requirements for The Perfect Date™: Windows 95 or Windows 98, 133MHz Pentium IBM-compatible PC, 16MB RAM, 40MB available hard disk space (C:), 640 × 480 256 color resolution (small fonts), CD-ROM drive, Windows-compatible sound card, mouse, or Windows-compatible pointing device. 800 × 600 High Color or True Color resolution is recommended.

She's got a computer, but it's no fun. The solution?

The Perfect Date™

A CD-ROM for women who have Windows 95/98

We've all been there. You go out on a blind date, which turns out so mismatched and awful that months later you're laughing hysterically at how preposterous the whole thing was. Well, now you can skip the horrifying "live through it" stage and go right to the fun with The Perfect Date™, an interactive novelty on CD-ROM for women who have a computer running Windows 95/98.

Rendered in beautiful watercolor illustrations, The Perfect Date™ begins when you meet your date at a restaurant and find yourself in conversation with a man (and we use that term loosely) who, depending on the questions you ask, puts his personalities right on display. Mamma's Boy, Sugar Daddy, Punk Rocker—all of these and more does he become as he tries his dysfunctional best to win your heart. Also along for the ride are your waiter and the restaurant's patrons, which include the local drunk and a lady advisor (should you need help relating to your dinner companion).

Give The Perfect Date™ to a friend or go on The Perfect Date™ yourself!
All copies come with a 30-day money-back guarantee!

Three ways to purchase The Perfect Date™

1. **Order online at www.size-eight.com**

   Free shipping and handling for online orders means you get The Perfect Date™ for only $14.95 per copy!

2. **Fax the coupon below to (603) 994-4725**

   Each copy costs $17.95, which includes a $3 s/h fee.

3. **Mail the coupon below to Size Eight Software**

   Each copy costs $17.95, which includes a $3 s/h fee.

To order The Perfect Date™ (@ $17.95/copy), mail this coupon to: Size Eight Software, Cherokee Station, P.O. Box 20735, New York, NY 10021-0074. We cannot accept cash or personal checks. Please allow two to three weeks for delivery.

Payment Method: _____Visa _____ MasterCard_____ American Express _____ Money Order

Credit Card #: _____ Number of copies ordered:_____

For credit card payment, authorize with your signature: _____

Name _____ Email address _____

Address _____

City _____ State _____ Zip Code _____

Minimum system requirements for The Perfect Date™: Windows 95 or Windows 98, 133MHz Pentium IBM-compatible PC, 16MB RAM, 40MB available hard disk space (C:), 640 × 480 256 color resolution (small fonts), CD-ROM drive, Windows-compatible sound card, mouse, or Windows-compatible pointing device. 800 × 600 High Color or True Color resolution is recommended.